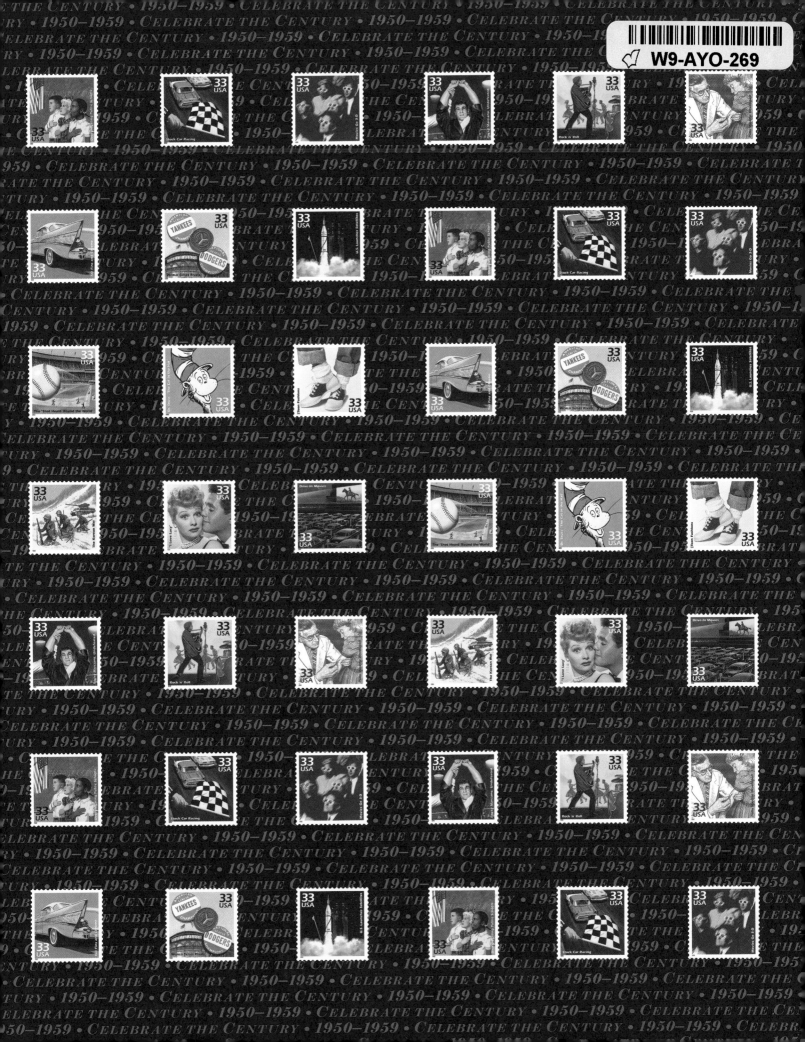

Celebrate
THE Century™

A COLLECTION OF
COMMEMORATIVE STAMPS

1950-1959

PUT YOUR STAMP
ON HISTORY
1 9 0 0 ▪ 2 0 0 0

UNITED STATES POSTAL SERVICE

UNITED STATES POSTAL SERVICE

POSTMASTER GENERAL
AND CHIEF EXECUTIVE OFFICER
William J. Henderson

CHIEF MARKETING OFFICER
Allen Kane

EXECUTIVE DIRECTOR, STAMP SERVICES
Azeezaly S. Jaffer

MANAGER, STAMP MARKETING
Gary A. Thuro

PROJECT MANAGER
Patsy L. Laws

TIME-LIFE BOOKS IS A DIVISION OF TIME LIFE INC.

TIME-LIFE CUSTOM PUBLISHING

VICE PRESIDENT AND PUBLISHER
Terry Newell

VICE PRESIDENT OF
SALES AND MARKETING
Neil Levin

DIRECTOR OF NEW PRODUCT DEVELOPMENT
Teresa Graham

PROJECT COORDINATOR
Jennifer L. Ward

PRINTING PRODUCTION MANAGER
Carolyn M. Clark

EDITORIAL STAFF FOR CELEBRATE THE CENTURY

MANAGING EDITOR
Morin Bishop

EDITORS
John Bolster, Eve Peterson

DESIGNERS
Barbara Chilenskas, Jia Baek

WRITERS
Theresa Deal, Rachael Nevins

RESEARCHER
Ward Calhoun

PHOTO EDITOR
Bill Broyles

First printing. Printed in U.S.A.

TIME-LIFE is a trademark of Time Warner Inc. U.S.A.

LIBRARY OF CONGRESS CATALOGING-IN-PUBLICATION DATA
Celebrate the century: a collection of commemorative stamps.
p. cm. Includes index.
Contents: v. 6. 1950–1959
ISBN 0-7835-5522-6
1. Commemorative postage stamps—United States—History—20th century.
2. United States—History—20th century.
I. Time-Life Books

HE6185.U5C45 1998 97–46952
769.56973—DC21 CIP

Books produced by Time-Life Custom Publishing are available at a special bulk discount for promotional and premium use. Custom adaptations can also be created to meet your specific marketing goals. Call 1-800-323-5255.

PICTURE CREDITS

Cover, Elvis Presley Enterprises, Inc.; 4, Globe Photos; 5, Brown Brothers; 6, UPI/Corbis-Bettmann; 7, UPI/Corbis-Bettmann; 8, UPI/Corbis-Bettmann; 9, Archive Photos; 10, Elvis Presley Enterprises, Inc.; 11, UPI/Corbis-Bettmann; 12, top, Michael Ochs Archives/Venice, CA.; inset, Popperfoto/Archive Photos; bottom, UPI/Corbis-Bettmann; 13, UPI/Corbis-Bettmann; 14, top, Archive Photos; inset, Brown Brothers; 15, both, Michael Ochs Archives/Venice, CA.; 16, Jet Propulsion Laboratory; 17, Marshall Space Flight Center; 18, top left, Sovfoto/ Eastfoto; inset, Archive Photos; bottom, Sovfoto/Eastfoto; 19, Associated Press; 20, left, NASA; right, UPI/Corbis-Bettmann; 21, top, NASA Langley Research Center; bottom, Superstock; 22, Transcendental Graphics; 23, top, UPI/Corbis-Bettmann; stamp, Major League Baseball trademarks and copyrights are used with permission of Major League Baseball Properties, Inc; 24, Transcendental Graphics; 25, UPI/Corbis-Bettmann; 26, both, Transcendental Graphics; 27, *Daily Mirror*/Corbis-Bettmann; 28, Superstock; 29, Tony Stone; 30, top, Corbis-Bettmann; bottom left, Archive Photos; bottom right, Superstock; 31, top left, UPI/Corbis-Bettmann; top right, Baldwin H. Ward/Corbis; bottom, Archive Photos; 32, Minnesota Historical Society; 33, top, Barson Collection/Archive Photos; bottom, Corbis-Bettmann; 34, Globe Photos; 35, top, Photofest; stamp, Images of Lucille Ball and Desi Arnaz are used with permission of Desilu, too, LLC. *I Love Lucy* is a registered trademark of CBS Inc.; 36, Desilu, too; 37, top, Bill Broyles Collection; bottom, Globe Photos; 38, Culver Pictures; 39, left, Archive Photos; right, Bill Broyles Collection; 40, J.R. Eyerman/*Life*/Corbis-Bettmann; 42, left, Photofest; right, Archive Photos; 43, both, Photofest; 44, both, Photofest; 45, UPI/Corbis-Bettmann; 46, UPI/Corbis-Bettmann; 47, UPI/Corbis-Bettmann; 48, UPI/Corbis-Bettmann; 49, both, UPI/Corbis-Bettmann; 50, left, Archive Photos; 50-51, UPI/Corbis-Bettmann; 51, inset, UPI/Corbis-Bettmann; 52, UPI/Corbis-Bettmann; 53, *Daily Mirror*/Corbis-Bettmann; 54, UPI/Corbis-Bettmann; 55, both, UPI/Corbis-Bettmann; 56, UPI/Corbis-Bettmann; 57, top, UPI/Corbis-Bettmann; left, UPI/Corbis-Bettmann; right, Meyer Liebowitz/*New York Times*/Archive Photos; 58, UPI/Corbis-Bettmann; 59, UPI/Corbis-Bettmann; 60, top, UPI/Corbis-Bettmann; inset, Bern Keating/Black Star; 61, left, UPI/Corbis-Bettmann; right, Photofest; 62, UPI/Corbis-Bettmann; 63, Tames/*New York Times*/Archive Photos; 64, Superstock; 65, March of Dimes Birth Defects Foundation; 66, left, Brown Brothers; center, Brown Brothers; right, AP/Wide World Photos; 67, left, Brown Brothers; center, AP/Wide World Photos; right, UPI/Corbis-Bettmann; 68, *Daily Mirror*/Corbis-Bettmann; 69, top, UPI/Corbis-Bettmann; stamp, Major League Baseball trademarks and copyrights are used with permission of Major League Baseball Properties, Inc; 70, inset, UPI/Corbis-Bettmann; bottom, UPI/Corbis-Bettmann; 71, top, UPI/Corbis-Bettmann; bottom, National Baseball Hall of Fame Library, Cooperstown, NY; 72, top, UPI/Corbis-Bettmann; inset, National Baseball Hall of Fame Library, Cooperstown, NY; 73, both, UPI/Corbis-Bettmann; 74, UPI/Corbis-Bettmann; 75, Sam Falk/*New York Times*/Archive Photos; 76, UPI/Corbis-Bettmann; 77, top, Hulton Getty/Tony Stone; inset, UPI/Corbis-Bettmann; 78, top, from *The American Drive-in Movie Theater*; middle, UPI/Corbis-Bettmann; bottom, from *The American Drive-in Movie Theater*; 79, UPI/Corbis-Bettmann; 80, Underwood Photo Archives, SF; 81, UPI/Corbis-Bettmann; 82, Archive Photos; 83, top left, Underwood Photo Archives, SF; top right, Superstock; bottom, *Daily Mirror*/Corbis-Bettmann; 84, top, Michael Ochs Archives/Venice, CA.; inset, UPI/Corbis-Bettmann; 85, Globe Photos; 86, Daytona Racing Archives; 87, Daytona Racing Archives; 88, top, UPI/Corbis-Bettmann; bottom left, Archive Photos; bottom right, UPI/Corbis-Bettmann; 89, UPI/Corbis-Bettmann; 90, top, Daytona Racing Archives; inset, Hulton Getty/Liaison; 91, UPI/Corbis-Bettmann; 92, Courtesy Random House; 93, top, Courtesy Random House; stamp, *The Cat in the Hat*®™ Dr. Seuss Enterprises, LP, 1957. All rights reserved; 94, Theodor Geisel Collection, Mandeville Special Collections Library, University of California, San Diego; 95, John Bryson.

CONTENTS

The '50s saw U.S. GIs fight in Korea (left) and a new generation (above) thrill to the sounds of rock 'n' roll.

INTRODUCTION

The popular conception of the 1950s is as an era of cookie-cutter conformity, black-and-white morality and an overriding, *Father Knows Best* blandness. The 1998 film *Pleasantville*, which depicted the decade as having taken place literally in black and white, attests to this received perception. It's an interpretation that gains momentum when the '50s are viewed alongside the psychedelic glare of the '60s, but in truth it is a misconception. Scratch beneath the Bryl-creamed surface of America in the '50s and you'll find a surprisingly turbulent, dynamic era that prefigured the course the world would follow to the century's end. It's easy to forget that the teen rebel was invented in the '50s, not the '60s. James Dean and Marlon Brando, rock 'n' roll and the early civil rights movement are as much a part of the '50s as Ward and June and the Beaver are.

True to its paradoxical nature, the decade began in unprecedented prosperity, but with real danger lurking abroad. Most Americans, however, didn't want to hear about any new threats to the free world. World War II was behind them and bright economic prospects were ahead. The population boomed, the economy and the middle class expanded in lockstep and most Americans adopted a staunchly isolationist attitude where international affairs were concerned. Events in the Far East may as well have been taking place on the moon.

But the Soviet Union, the United States's former ally, which had played a crucial role in the victory over the Nazis, was becoming increasingly expansionist. Buttressed by the revolution in China, which put Mao Zedong in charge of the globe's most populous nation in 1949, the Soviets seemed, to the West at least, to be enter-

Federal troops were needed to escort the first black students into Little Rock's Central High.

---

some 35,000 U.S. servicemen, one million Chinese soldiers and three million Koreans, civilians and soldiers alike, a devastating one-tenth of the peninsula's population. The war also solidified the polar positions of the United States and the Soviet Union as implacable enemies in the Cold War. Though horribly brutal, the Korean War was mercifully brief. When it ended on July 27, 1953, the Korean map had not been redrawn—on the contrary, the peninsula remained divided exactly as it had been before the conflict, roughly in half, along the 38th parallel—but the nascent United Nations had established itself as a legitimate peacekeeping force in the world, and the United States had demonstrated its resolve in the face of communist expansion.

At home, Americans focused on far more light-hearted pursuits. A brash new music, which grew out of rhythm and blues, burst onto the scene in mid-decade and quickly seized the undivided attention of America's youth. The original rock 'n' roll supernova, a white country boy from East Tupelo, Mississippi, named Elvis Presley, took his cues from black musicians who came before him, such as Arthur Crudup and Ray Charles, but he was also influenced by country and gospel. His records "crossed over"; that is, they appealed to both blacks and whites. African-American artists such as Little Richard and Chuck Berry also pioneered the new style and, though not as successful as Presley, were also able to attract both black and white audiences. While Berry's rock 'n' roll had a country tinge, Presley's first records were considered "too black" for white radio stations and "too country" for black stations. While not exactly merging, the two cultures were definitely cross-pollinating.

In 1954 the Supreme Court handed down a landmark decision that compelled, albeit with great practical difficulty, black and white cultures

taining visions of a communist world. Western governments' fears of communist aggression grew even more acute after the Soviets staged their first successful test of an atomic bomb in August 1949.

Although many Americans tried to ignore these developments, President Harry Truman and his administration kept a close eye on them. In 1950 U.S. secretary of state Dean Acheson made a speech enumerating the regions that America would defend from communist aggression. Out of mere carelessness, Acheson did not include South Korea and Taiwan. Sure enough, later that year forces from communist North Korea, equipped with Soviet arms, and in some cases advised by Soviet officers, invaded the U.S.-backed South, intent on uniting the Korean peninsula under communist rule.

The conflict that followed claimed the lives of

The Yankees (on the field) and the Dodgers met in the World Series four times in the '50s.

to come together. In the case of *Brown v. the Board of Education of Topeka, Kansas,* a group of lawsuits that challenged the nation's racially segregated public school systems, the Court ruled that segregation was inherently discriminatory and therefore unconstitutional.

The decision was a powerful statement by the highest court in the land, but implementing its mandate in the South proved to be another, more difficult matter. Some states fought desegregation with red tape, mobilizing every conceivable bureaucratic weapon at their disposal to prevent black and white students from occupying the same classrooms. Other states were more brazen. Orval Faubus, the governor of Arkansas, summoned the National Guard on September 4, 1957, to prevent nine black students from entering Little Rock's Central High School on the first day of school. After

a three-week standoff, President Dwight Eisenhower deployed the 101st Airborne Division to escort the students through the angry mob of whites who had gathered outside the school.

Public school desegregation was a critical early step in the ongoing process of achieving social justice for the nation's African-American citizens. Another significant barrier had fallen in 1947, when Jackie Robinson became the first African-American to compete in Major League Baseball. Larry Doby of the Cleveland Indians would follow him, and by the 1950s, black ballplayers were commonplace in the majors. Perhaps not coincidentally, the game enjoyed a golden era in the 1950s, with the locus of power squarely fixed in New York. The Big Apple was home to three franchises, the Dodgers, the Yankees and the Giants, and all three were stocked with Hall of

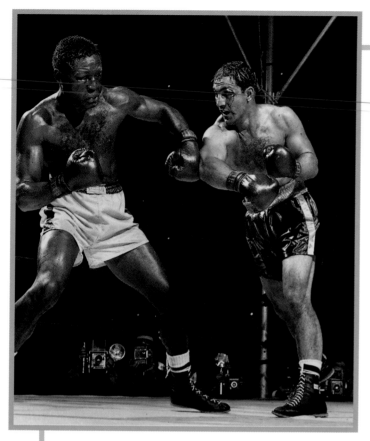

Marciano (above right, against Ezzard Charles) retired as history's only unbeaten heavyweight champ.

Fame talent. New York sent a team to the World
Series every year from 1949 to 1958, with the
Yankees and Dodgers meeting in the Fall Classic
five times in that span. The mighty Yankees won
six titles during the '50s. In 1951 the Giants ral-
lied from 13½ games back on August 11 and
caught the Dodgers at the end of the regular season. They then miraculously defeated them on
Bobby Thomson's Shot Heard 'Round the World
in the bottom of the ninth of the final game of a
three-game playoff. A reversal-of-fortune blast,
Thomson's three-run homer remains a where-
were-you-when moment for legions of fans, not
only in New York but also nationwide.

Another athlete with national appeal, though
nowhere more beloved than in the Boston area,
was boxer Rocky Marciano. A hard-punching
heavyweight with an unorthodox, lunging style,

Marciano was known as "The Brockton Blockbuster." Once described by sportswriter Red Smith
as having "a right hand that registered nine on
the Richter scale," Marciano won 49 bouts without a loss in his eight-year pro career, 43 of them
by knockout. On September 23, 1952, he defeated
Jersey Joe Walcott for the heavyweight championship, a title he defended six times before retir-
ing in 1956. His perfect record remains intact and
unmatched to this day.

In the South, a wild auto racing circuit
emerged, steeped in "good old boy" bootleg culture, and with a marquee track literally on the
beach in Daytona Beach, Florida. The pioneers of
stock car racing took no prisoners, and often, no
purses, as corrupt early promoters frequently
hightailed it with the prize money before the
races were finished. But upon its incorporation in
1948, the National Association for Stock Car
Automobile Racing (NASCAR) buffed the sport's
image—a little. Racers remained rapscallions—
one early competitor, Tim Flock, drove nine races
with his pet rhesus monkey, Jocko Flocko, riding
shotgun—and cheating was commonplace, but
rabid fan interest and, later, corporate sponsorships eventually transformed the sport into the
multimillion-dollar enterprise it is today.

That transformation coincided with a surging
American economy, which created greater leisure
and more abundant wealth than the nation had
ever seen. The burgeoning bourgeoisie meant
that, for the first time in U.S. history, young people
had a surplus of free time and the financial
wherewithal to take advantage of it. Teenagers
quickly generated—or marketers generated for
them, depending on your point of view—a culture unto themselves. Hordes of teenagers dressed
in the latest styles—bobbysocks, puffy, appliquéd
skirts and pedal pushers for the girls; cuffed blue
jeans, T-shirts and slicked-back hair for the

boys—crowded into soda shops, cruised around in their parents' oversized chrome-covered cars or smooched their way through the latest 3-D horror flick at their local drive-in. Young people as the predominant consumers of American culture were here to stay.

Teenagers weren't the only ones having fun in the prosperous '50s. On the television, which had only recently become a common household item, Americans of all ages tuned in to a zany redhead named Lucille Ball. Along with her husband, the bandleader Desi Arnaz, Ball starred in *I Love Lucy*, the first show to be shot on film in front of an audience, and the first situation comedy in TV history to top the overall ratings. In fact, *Lucy* seized the No. 1 spot four times in its six-year run, and remains a favorite in syndication today.

Children were entertained by the high jinks of Dr. Seuss's *The Cat in the Hat*, which debuted in 1957 and introduced an element of irrepressible mischief into children's literature. But children of the '50s could not be as carefree as children of later decades—especially in the summertime, when a deadly, crippling virus called poliomyelitis raged. Mothers feared sending their children into crowded public spaces such as swimming pools and movie theaters lest they catch the highly contagious virus. In the summer of 1952, while the country was experiencing its worst polio epidemic ever, a young virologist named Jonas Salk was developing a vaccine for the virus. Field-tested on more than a million schoolchildren on April 26, 1954, the vaccine was pronounced safe and effective the following year, and Salk became a household name.

As soon as Salk's vaccine quelled the fears of disease within, the space race between the Soviet Union and the United States gave Americans a new cause for concern from without, in this case from the once-innocent skies above. The competition began in earnest in mid-decade, with the

Lucille Ball (above, right) and Desi Arnaz created one of television's most enduring shows.

Eisenhower administration's pronouncement that the United States would seek to launch an information-gathering satellite by the end of 1958. America was beaten to the heavens, however, by the Soviet Union, which launched *Sputnik* in October 1957. The United States evened the score with the launch of *Explorer I* in January 1958 and ensured that it would remain at the forefront of space exploration when Congress established NASA in the summer of '58. The organization's first order of business would be the sending of humans into outer space.

That was a challenge for the next decade, when all the complexity seething beneath the surface of the 1950s would sprout across the cultural landscape. The '60s, like the '50s, would begin with a military conflict (whose roots stretched to the mid-'50s) but few Americans would ignore this one—and all would discover that policing the world was a far more complicated task than anyone had anticipated.

ROCK 'N' ROLL

Music producer Quincy Jones has said that rock 'n' roll started the moment 21-year-old Elvis Presley appeared on *Stage Show*, the Dorsey brothers' television program, in 1956. Before then, the pop charts had been dominated by sweater-clad, straight-arrow crooners like Perry Como and Bing Crosby. When the leering, sneering Presley took the stage to hiccup and hip-swivel his way through "Shake, Rattle, and Roll," the crooners vanished, buried beneath the squeals of a million teenage girls. Pop music, not to mention American culture, would never be the same again.

Some 54 million people—82.6 percent of the television audience—would witness an appearance by Presley on Ed Sullivan's *Toast of the Town* later that year, and not all of them were as thrilled as the orgiastic studio audiences. The new music was rebellious and overtly sexual—its name, coined in 1954 by Cleveland disc jockey

Alan Freed, came from a risqué blues lyric: "My baby rocks me with a steady roll"—and the older generation was scandalized. To them, Presley was a vulgar menace. "He can't last," said comedian Jackie Gleason. "I tell you flatly—he can't last."

Of course Elvis not only lasted, but—as Gleason's alter ego Ralph Kramden might have put it—he went "to the moon." Presley made 11 gold records in 1956, sold more than 480,000,000 copies of his records before his death in 1977 and spent 24 consecutive years on the charts, a feat unsurpassed to this day.

He single-handedly launched rock 'n' roll into the stratosphere, but Presley was by no means the architect of the music. He borrowed from a variety of sources for his sound, including blues, country, gospel and rockabilly. His first single, "That's All Right (Mama)," was written by bluesman Arthur Crudup, and the B-side, "Blue Moon of Kentucky," was a Bill Monroe bluegrass number.

Presley's electric stage presence (left) provoked throngs of teens (above) wherever he appeared.

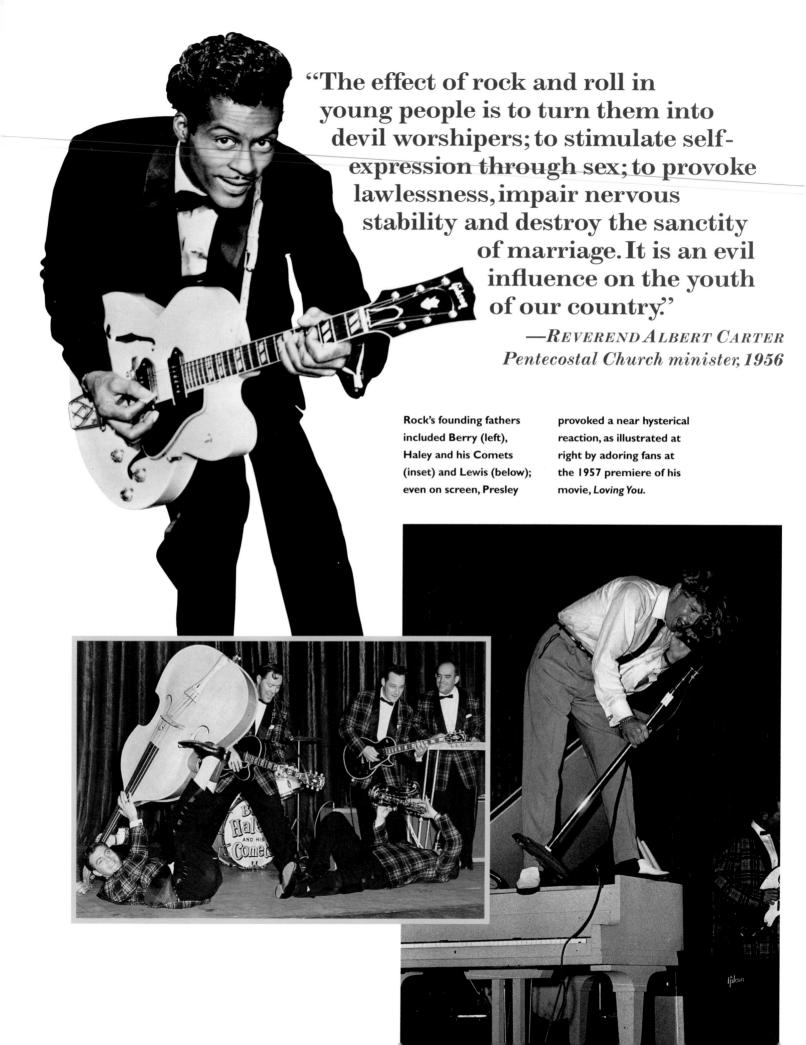

"The effect of rock and roll in young people is to turn them into devil worshipers; to stimulate self-expression through sex; to provoke lawlessness, impair nervous stability and destroy the sanctity of marriage. It is an evil influence on the youth of our country."

—*REVEREND ALBERT CARTER*
Pentecostal Church minister, 1956

Rock's founding fathers included Berry (left), Haley and his Comets (inset) and Lewis (below); even on screen, Presley provoked a near hysterical reaction, as illustrated at right by adoring fans at the 1957 premiere of his movie, *Loving You.*

And while the 19-year-old Presley was cutting these first tracks at Memphis's Sun Studios in 1954, rock 'n' roll was sprouting—like a weed, the older generation no doubt would have said—all over the country.

In Macon, Georgia, a flamboyant piano player named Richard Wayne Penniman blended boogie-woogie with rhythm and blues to create his rocking sound. Calling himself Little Richard, he sported a wild pompadour and sang in a howling falsetto about "Long Tall Sally," and "Tutti Frutti." In St. Louis, Chuck Berry, who had a day job as a beautician, released a single called "Maybellene." Part blues, part country, the song was filled with sly, witty lyrics about cars and girls. It became a Top Ten hit as well as the blueprint for

Berry's influential style. Berry topped his act off with trademark double-string guitar licks and a signature "duckwalk" strut. He was so seminal a figure that when he toured the country later in his career, he could travel alone, picking up a backup band in each city along the way. He rightly assumed that any musician playing rock 'n' roll had honed his chops on Chuck Berry tunes.

Other important pioneers included pianist Fats Domino of New Orleans, who outsold every other '50s rocker save Elvis; Buddy Holly of Lubbock, Texas, who recorded an indelible catalog of songs before his death in a plane crash at age 22; and Presley's Sun labelmate Jerry Lee Lewis, whose 1957 hit, "Great Balls of Fire," sold five million copies. Bill Haley and the Comets were the first

13

rock 'n' rollers to make the *Billboard* pop chart, with "Crazy Man Crazy" in 1953, and their signature tune, "Rock Around the Clock," reached No. 1 in 1955.

From coast to coast the new style took hold. Mainstream America was loosening up, rocking out. Indeed, it has often been said that rock 'n' roll, with its melting pot of musical antecedents and its rebellious and democratic nature—anyone can (and will) try it—is a metaphor for American culture. And Presley's poor-country-boy-hits-the-big-time story is the ultimate realization of the American Dream. When Elvis reappeared on Sullivan's show in January 1957, the host mandated that the star be filmed strictly from the waist up, the better to censor his rampant carnality. But it made no difference; rock 'n' roll was here to stay.

Dick Clark's popular television show, *American Bandstand* (top), helped draw unprecedented crowds into record stores **(opposite, above) in search of the latest releases from artists such as Little Richard (inset) and Buddy Holly (opposite, below).**

Aftermath

Rock 'n' roll received its second big boost in the 1960s with the British Invasion led by the Beatles and the Rolling Stones. Having cut their teeth on Chuck Berry, Little Richard and Fats Domino records, the shaggy-haired Beatles took the music to another level, expanding the possibilities and meaning of rock 'n' roll to a breadth previously unimagined. The Stones, inspired by Chicago blues, played a more straight-forward, raunchy rock 'n' roll, though not without ironic and envelope-pushing lyrics. After stagnating in the arena- and "progressive-" rock sounds of the '70s, rock 'n' roll was revitalized by punk and rap. Today, the music continues to remake itself, spawn hybrids and play a vital role in American culture.

U.S. ENTERS SPACE AGE

The space race between the United States and the Soviet Union began in earnest on July 29, 1955, when James Hagerty, President Eisenhower's press secretary, formally announced "that the President has approved plans by this country for going ahead with the launching of small orbiting satellites as part of the United States' participation in the International Geophysical Year," a worldwide study of geological and atmospheric phenomena. Artificial satellites would greatly assist the scientists in their research and mapmaking for the International Geophysical Year (IGY) by collecting data on solar activity and on the earth, its oceans and its atmosphere.

The United States was the first nation to announce its plans to launch a satellite, but on October 4, 1957, the Soviet Union became the first to actually launch one. Weighing only 183 pounds, measuring just 22 inches in diameter, and harm-

lessly beeping a radio transmission at regular intervals, *Sputnik* nonetheless stirred an anxiety in Americans that NASA chief historian Roger Launius has compared with the panic that followed the bombing of Pearl Harbor. The territory that had been invaded, of course, was not American soil: It was the heavens themselves. "Now, somehow, in some new way, the sky seemed almost alien," then Senate Majority Leader Lyndon B. Johnson later recalled. "I also remember the profound shock of realizing that it might be possible for another nation to achieve technological superiority over this great country of ours."

Sputnik not only shook America's confidence in the technology and industries that had generated the postwar economic boom so critical to the growing middle class, it also exposed the nation's underlying sense of vulnerability. Indeed, in some ways the Cold War had less to do with the conflict-

The *Explorer I* (left) was engineered by James Pickering, James Van Allen and Werner von Braun (top, left to right).

17

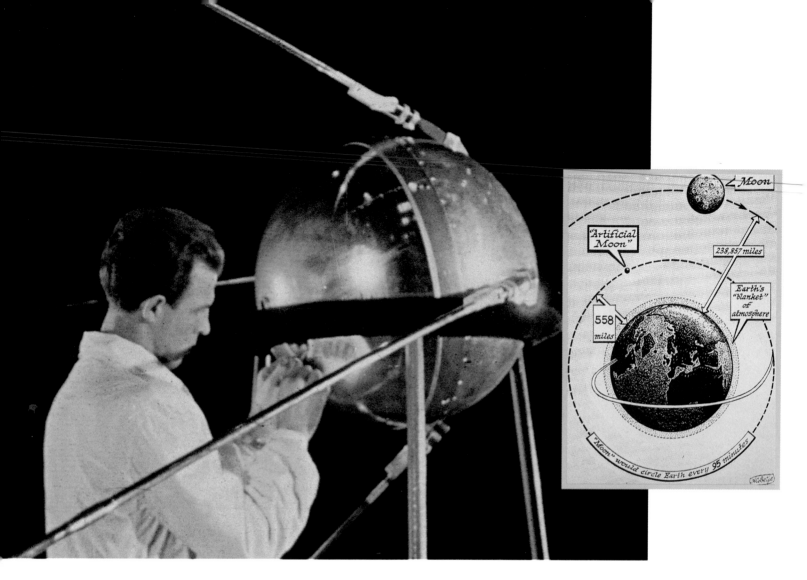

The launching of *Sputnik* (above) into a carefully planned orbit (inset) motivated Americans across the country to train their telescopes on the sky (opposite) in hopes of catching a glimpse of the Soviet satellite; Laika aboard *Sputnik II* (right) became the first living creature to orbit the earth.

"One small ball in the air, something that does not raise my apprehension, not one iota."

—PRESIDENT EISENHOWER, on the launching of Sputnik, 1957

ing ideologies of the United States and the Soviet Union than it did with the potential for devastation that the development of nuclear weapons engendered. And if the Soviet Union could successfully launch a satellite, it also could likely produce an intercontinental ballistic missile.

For three months *Sputnik* whizzed around the globe once every 96 minutes, and on November 3, 1957, it was joined by *Sputnik II*, a heavier, more sophisticated satellite that carried a dog, Laika, the first living creature to orbit the earth. Meanwhile, in an attempt to soothe American fears, the White House announced that on December 6, 1957, the United States would test-launch a rocket, as a part of Project Vanguard, its satellite development program for the IGY. The media were invited to witness—and, presumably, cele-

brate—the event, which turned out to be a disaster: The rocket traveled only four feet into the air before bursting into flames.

Project Vanguard, however, was not the United States's only rocket development program. Since the late '40s, in fact, the Army Ballistic Missile Agency—a group of scientists, many of them German engineers who had developed the V2 flying bombs for the Nazis during World War II—had been testing rockets at White Sands Missile Range in New Mexico. In the early '50s the group proposed to launch a satellite with one of its Jupiter C missiles, but because Eisenhower wished to emphasize the peaceful applications of space technology, the Defense Department rejected the agency's proposal in favor of the Vanguard project, which, unlike the Jupiter C plan, had been

From the ashes of the failed Vanguard launch (right), which was intended to launch a test satellite (above), emerged the Mercury program and the first seven U.S. astronauts (opposite, above), Alan Shepard, Virgil "Gus" Grissom and L. Gordon Cooper (back row, left to right), and Walter Schirra, Donald "Deke" Slayton, John Glenn and Scott Carpenter (front row, left to right), along with a rededication in American classrooms (opposite, below) to math and science.

designed and developed for scientific purposes alone.

With the first Vanguard launch gone "kaputnik" (as some nicknamed the ill-fated attempt), Secretary of Defense Neil McElroy gave the go-ahead to the Jupiter C team. On the night of January 31, 1958, *Explorer I* was successfully launched from Cape Canaveral, Florida. A cylinder only 80 inches long and weighing just 31 pounds, it carried a Geiger counter designed by James A. Van Allen, a physicist at the University of Iowa, to measure the radiation surrounding the earth. This small instrument made one of the biggest discoveries of the IGY: belts of high-energy particles trapped by the earth's magnetic field. And on

March 17, 1958, a successful Vanguard launch went up and gathered more data on what became known as the Van Allen Radiation Belts.

The crisis of confidence that *Sputnik* caused was now over, and the United States acted quickly to ensure that no further ventures by the Soviet Union into outer space would set off another. In the summer of 1958, Congress passed the National Aeronautics and Space Act, which established a civilian organization with the mandate to "plan, direct and conduct aeronautical and space activities." NASA opened its doors on October 1, 1958, and immediately set to work on its first project: to send humans into outer space.

Aftermath

Explorer I remained in orbit until 1967, and through 1984 sixty-four more Explorer satellites were launched to collect data on phenomena including magnetic fields, solar wind and ultraviolet radiation. Hundreds more commercial, scientific and military satellites now orbit the earth and facilitate telecommunications and navigation as well as meteorological, geophysical and astrophysical study. The Mir space station, launched in 1986 by the Soviet Union, is also in earth's orbit. The space race long over, American and Russian scientists now collaborate in their research.

SHOT HEARD 'ROUND THE WORLD

On October 3, 1951, New York Giants third base-man Bobby Thomson hit the most famous home run in baseball history. The blast, which defeated the Brooklyn Dodgers for the National League pennant, became known as the Shot Heard 'Round the World. Sportswriter Red Smith called it the Miracle of Coogan's Bluff (Coogan's Bluff overlooked the Giants' home field, the Polo Grounds). Writer Don DeLillo used the dramatic moment as the opening scene of his epic historical novel, *Underworld.* It functions as the closing act to an innocent era, before the Cold War and the Bomb took center stage, before the black-and-white world got swallowed up by a murky, morally ambiguous field of gray.

The "Shot Heard 'Round the World"

Attending the game—in real life—were such luminaries as Walter Winchell, Frank Sinatra, Jackie Gleason, Toots Shor and FBI chief J. Edgar Hoover. And as definitive proof that there was something in the air that day, the latter four—

three parts showbiz, one part G-man—were sitting together. Sinatra, Gleason, Shor and Hoover shared a box behind the Giants dugout, along the third baseline. With the Dodgers holding a 1–0 lead through six innings, DeLillo imagines Shor telling Gleason, a Brooklyn fan, that he's not worried. "It's only one-zip. The Giants didn't come from 13½ games back just to blow it on the last day. This is the miracle year. Nobody has a vocabulary for what happened this year."

Indeed, nobody does, but in so many inadequate words, it went as follows: Entering the 1951 season the Giants were favored to win the National League pennant. Their lineup was stocked with talented players, including short-stop Alvin Dark, outfielder Monte Irvin, third baseman Thomson, and leadoff man and second baseman Eddie (Brat) Stanky. Their top pitch-ers, Sal Maglie and Larry Jansen, each would win 23 games in '51. Contrary to the lofty expec-

Two sides to the miracle: Branca and Jackie Robinson (left) mourn; Thomson, Jansen and Maglie (top, left to right) celebrate.

Stanky (left, in jacket) and Durocher celebrate as Thomson rounded third base, to be greeted at the plate (above) by his exultant Giants teammates.

tations, however, the Giants followed a season-opening victory with 11 straight losses and plummeted to last place. After making a few personnel changes, including the promotion from the minors of a young center fielder named Willie Mays, the Giants began to right themselves. They reached .500 by the end of May, and slowly but surely gained ground on their hated cross-river rivals, the first-place Dodgers, whose stalwarts included Duke Snider, Roy Campanella, Gil Hodges, and on the mound, their own pair of 20-game winners, control artist Preacher Roe and hard-throwing intimidator Don Newcombe. But Brooklyn swept the Giants in a three-game series in early July, and New York fell 7½ games behind. "We knocked 'em out," said Dodgers manager Chuck Dressen. "They'll never bother us again." A Giants' loss to Philadelphia and a Brooklyn victory over the

"The art of fiction is dead. Reality has strangled invention. Only the utterly impossible, the inexpressibly fantastic, can ever be plausible again."

—*RED SMITH,*
columnist for
The New York Times

Braves in the first game of a doubleheader left the Giants 13½ games back on August 11.

The next day the Giants took two from Philadelphia and began a tremendous late-season surge. They won 16 in a row at the end of August and went on to win 37 of their last 44 games and caught the Dodgers with two games left in the season. Each team won its final two games and, with identical 96–58 records, met in a three-game playoff to decide which of them would go to the World Series. It was only the second such playoff in the 76-year history of the NL. They split the first two games and were deadlocked, 1–1, entering the eighth inning of the decider. The Dodgers touched New York ace Sal Maglie

for three runs in the top of the eighth, and it appeared that the Giants had indeed come all the way back only to blow it on the last day. Brooklyn took a 4–1 lead into the bottom of the ninth. The fireballing Newcombe looked all but unhittable. Giants fans started streaming toward the exits.

Those who remained stirred little when New York got a leadoff single in the ninth. The next batter laced a single the opposite way, however, and suddenly the Giants, with runners at the corners, had Newcombe on the ropes. After a foulout by Monte Irvin, the Giants' Whitey Lockman smacked a double to left field, driving in one run and putting men at second and third, one out, the Brooklyn lead down to 4–2.

With Newcombe (shown above in the 1956 World Series against the Yankees) cruising on the mound, the Dodgers seemed to have **the game in hand; Branca (top and opposite, left) became good friends with Thomson (opposite, right) in later years.**

In a move that Brooklyn fans argue about to this day, Dressen decided to pull Newcombe and replace him with 25-year-old Ralph Branca. A 13-game winner in '51, Branca would be entering the game with only one day's rest, having started—and lost—the first game of the series, 3–1, the key blow in the loss being a home run by none other than Thomson. Now a tired Branca was being asked to face Thomson again, in yet another critical situation. Many observers thought—with classic 20-20 hindsight—that Dressen should have stuck with Newcombe or perhaps gone with Carl Erskine, Brooklyn's talented right-hander who had won 16 games in '51.

Thomson stepped to the plate for New York and took a called strike. At the Baseball Hall of Fame in Cooperstown, New York, there is a glass case containing the bat, spikes and glove Thomson wore that day. On the side of the case there is a button visitors can press to hear the voice of radio

announcer Russ Hodges describing what followed. "Branca throws ... there's a long drive.... It's gonna be ... I believe.... The Giants win the pennant! The Giants win the pennant! The Giants win the pennant! The Giants win the pennant! Bobby Thomson hits it into the lower deck of the left field stands. The Giants win the pennant and they're going crazy. They're going crazy. I don't believe it. I don't believe it. I do *NOT* believe it."

The Polo Grounds erupted into delirious pandemonium as Thomson circled the bases. The irrepressible Stanky leaped onto the back of manager Leo Durocher and the pair cantered down the third baseline in wild celebration. Thomson was mobbed by his happy teammates at home plate. In the stands long suffering Giants fans, who had not seen their proud franchise win a pennant since 1937, wept openly.

Aftermath

Riding the momentum of their dramatic playoff victory, the Giants won two of the first three games of the 1951 World Series against the Yankees. They dropped the next three, however, and lost the Series four games to two. When the Giants returned to the Fall Classic in '54 and swept Cleveland, Thomson was no longer on the team, having been traded to Milwaukee at the start of the season.

Branca, too, had been traded by the time the Dodgers broke through to World Series glory in '55. The former 20-game winner struggled to come to terms with his role in the Miracle of Coogan's Bluff and had only two more winning seasons after '51.

Forever linked by their roles in the drama, Thomson and Branca became friends and often appear in tandem at baseball memorabilia shows.

TAIL FINS AND CHROME

From the elegant to the outlandish, the designs of American automobiles in the 1950s reflected the brashness of the nation and its confidence in itself and its economy. The relationship between man and machine took on the heady, impractical fervor of a budding romance as the automobile industry's designers and advertisers encouraged Americans to think of their cars not simply as a means of transportation, but as an extension of the self, simultaneously expressing one's status in society and satisfying one's every fantasy.

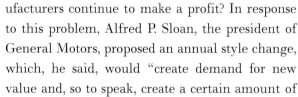

During the 1910s and '20s, Ford's development of assembly-line techniques of mass production made automobiles affordable for ordinary Americans. Indeed, by 1926 the majority of people who could afford a car already owned one, and the following year production and sales declined for the first time. How would man-

ufacturers continue to make a profit? In response to this problem, Alfred P. Sloan, the president of General Motors, proposed an annual style change, which, he said, would "create demand for new value and, so to speak, create a certain amount of dissatisfaction with past models as compared with the new one." In 1927 General Motors began introducing new models of its cars annually, and for the first time Americans bought more Chevrolets than Fords.

Not until after the country had weathered the deprivations of the Depression and World War II, however, did car design truly gain speed. Leading the way was General Motors chief of design Harley Earl, who before joining the "art and color department" at GM in 1927 had worked for nearly a decade customizing auto bodies for Hollywood celebrities—a pool of clients among

"A chorus girl coming, a fighter plane going," is one historian's take on the chrome-covered behemoths (above and left).

1954 Cadillac Eldorado

whom his decidedly unconservative sense of style flourished. Earl had aviation in mind in his approach to automobile design. During the war, he and a team of stylists took the opportunity to view—under strict security and from a distance of 30 feet—the Lockheed P-38 Lightning pursuit plane. Its paired engines, fuselages and tail fins found their way into the graceful design of the 1948 Cadillac in the form of "little humped taillights," as Cadillac designer William L. Mitchell called them.

"The taillamp treatment caught on widely, because ultimately Cadillac owners realized that it gave them an extra receipt for their money in the form of a visible prestige marking for an expensive car," said Earl. And each passing year saw greater emphasis on "visible prestige markings" on automobiles: chrome accents that became flashier and tail fins that grew higher, sharper, more flamboyant. Cars other than the Cadillac sprouted tail fins, too: Oldsmobile in 1949, Buick in '52, Chrysler in '55 and Studebaker in '56.

1957 Oldsmobile Golden Rocket "88" Sedan

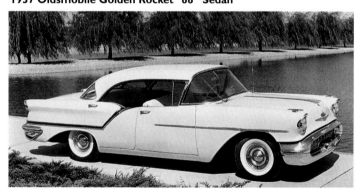

1958 Chrysler "300"

1955 Chevrolet Bel Aire

1956 Chrysler De Soto

"Is it responsible to camouflage one of America's most remarkable machines as a piece of gaudy merchandise?"

—RAYMOND LOEWY, former lead designer at Studebaker, 1955

With its allusion to a fighter plane, the tail fin suggested nothing but speed, an effect enhanced by the overall design: The square and upright look of pre-World War II automobiles had given way to the sleek, long, low look of the '50s. It has "the forward look of motion—even when it's stopped!" gushed admirers of the 1956 Chrysler in a television ad. But designers ultimately detracted from the speedy appearance by cluttering—and weighing down—cars with accessories. Perhaps the most absurd of these was the functionless pair

of bullet-shaped, chrome "Dagmars"—named after a big-breasted movie star—that started appearing on the front bumpers of Cadillacs in 1953. "A chorus girl coming, a fighter plane going," writes art historian Karal Ann Marling of the complete sex-and-violence package that the American automobile had become.

"I'd put smokestacks right in the middle of the sons of bitches if I thought I could sell more cars," Harley Earl cynically proclaimed. But smokestacks weren't necessary; General Motors was the

1959 Cadillac Fleetwood

largest, wealthiest company in the world, and the first to gross a billion dollars—despite the fact that Chrysler, among others, probably had superior engineering.

Habits change, though, and by 1957, in an unexpected twist, Americans were buying 79,000 no-frills Volkswagen Beetles annually. This was a sign of the more practical turn that automobile design would take in the future. Indeed, by the end of the decade Ford, Studebaker and even GM introduced their own lines of compact cars. Until then, however, Americans happily zoomed about on the interstate highway system—under construction since 1956—in their glorious gas-guzzling vehicles, which, when parked, also served as essential props at drive-in restaurants and movie theaters.

For '59...only Plymouth wagons give you so many luxury features...and low price, too!

Station wagons have reached an all-time peak in popularity, and the credit is largely Plymouth's. For no other wagon offers so much room, so many features at such low prices.

This year you get a choice of 10 great new wagons. You get all these Plymouth "firsts"—and more: Push-Button Power-Flite* or TorqueFlite* . . . easy-entry Swivel Seats* . . . safer

Total-Contact Brakes...new electronic Mirror-Matic Mirror* to end dangerous glare . . . new Automatic Beam Changer* . . . greatest glass area. Take a test drive today!

IF IT'S NEW, PLYMOUTH'S GOT IT!

REAR-FACING THIRD SEAT. The famous Plymouth first that lets third-seat passengers in or out without squirming past second seat. Big, comfortable, full-width—ample room for 3 adults.

BIGGEST OF THE LOW-PRICE FIELD. Plymouth wagons give you the most cargo space, most passenger room, plus the longest wheelbase. Second and third seats fold flush with floor, making level 10-foot loading deck.

NEW PUSH-BUTTON MASTER CONTROL CENTER puts you in complete command. Buttons at left control 3-speed Torque-Flite*, while those at right regulate heating, defrosting and ventilation. Instant Heater* delivers warm air in 30 seconds.

DISAPPEARING REAR WINDOW rolls up or down at the touch of a button. Operated either from driver's seat or from rear.

NEW CONSTANT LEVEL* TORSION-AIRE RIDE keeps your Plymouth wagon on an even keel no matter how heavy the load. Or choose famous Torsion-Aire. Ride at no extra cost.

'59 Plymouth

today's best buy...tomorrow's best trade

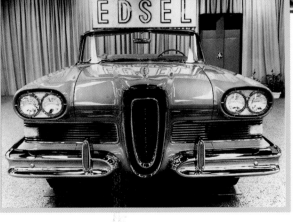

Chrome behemoths like the De Soto (opposite) were major gas guzzlers at the fuel pump; the '59 Plymouth wagon (top) was billed as a combination of luxury and practicality; Ford's Edsel (inset) was one chrome creation that bombed.

Aftermath

When the economy took a nosedive in 1958, Americans turned away from the gaudy new designs, a shift in consumer taste that produced one of the most notable failures in automotive history, the Ford Edsel.

The trend toward smaller, more fuel-efficient cars became pronounced during the '70s energy crisis, though the popularity in the '90s of gas-guzzling sports utility vehicles seems to indicate that Americans still have a passion for cars as large as their owners' egos.

I LOVE LUCY®

There have been few people in history who can be immediately identified by their first name. Even fewer can elicit a smile at the mere mention of that name. But ask just about anyone what comes to mind when they hear the name Lucy and almost every time they'll describe a certain brassy, red-lipped redhead whose antics kept generations of television viewers in hysterics. Lucille Ball had a true comedic gift and, along with her husband Desi Arnaz and a show called *I Love Lucy*®, she transformed the face of television comedy.

Lucille Ball and Desi Arnaz met on the set of the movie *Too Many Girls* in 1940 and after a whirlwind romance married later that year. Following their wedding, Desi resumed his career as a bandleader and film actor—though he was interrupted by a brief stint in the army—and Lucy continued to make movies. By the late '40s Lucy, now in her late 30s, saw more and more movie roles go to younger actresses, a situation that helped persuade her to take a job as the female lead on the CBS radio show *My Favorite Husband*. The show was performed before a live audience, and the role of Liz Cooper gave Lucy a chance to showcase her prodigious comic talents. By 1950 the show had become so successful that there was talk of bringing it to America's new favorite medium, television.

This was a busy period for Lucy and Desi, who formed their own company, Desilu Productions, to handle their far-flung entertainment interests. Lucy lobbied hard for Desi to play opposite her on the TV version of her radio show. CBS executives, reflecting the ongoing intolerance of white America, were concerned that the public wouldn't buy the premise of Lucy's character being married to a Cuban with an accent—this despite the fact that the two were actually married. To prove their chemistry as a couple and as a comedy team, Lucy and Desi put

Lucy's antics (left), and her chemistry with Vance, Frawley and Arnaz (top, left to right), made the show a runaway hit.

> ## "If we hadn't done anything else but bring that half-hour of fun, pleasure, and relaxation to most of the world, a world in such dire need of even that short time-out from its problems and sorrows, we should be content."
>
> —*DESI ARNAZ, in his autobiography,* **A Book,** *1976 (Desilu, too)*

together a vaudeville act and took it on the road. Their show was a success, and soon thereafter they began working on the pilot for what would eventually become *I Love Lucy®*. CBS granted the show, which was the first show filmed live in front of an audience, a slot in its fall lineup for 1951.

Many details of the show had to be ironed out quickly. Ball's and Arnaz's characters would be known as Lucy and Ricky Ricardo. Ricky would be a Cuban bandleader and Lucy his show-biz obsessed wife. The show also needed friends to interact with the Ricardos so Ball, Arnaz and writer/producer Jess Oppenheimer set out to cast the Ricardos' neighbors, the Mertzes. Veteran film actor William Frawley was brought in to play the tight-fisted yet good-natured Fred Mertz, and little-known stage and film actress Vivian Vance played his wife and Lucy's partner in crime, Ethel. It turned out to be inspired casting. Fred and Ethel were critical to many of the show's story lines that had Lucy and Ethel squaring off against Ricky and Fred in a battle of the sexes. Frawley and Vance reportedly didn't care much for each other off

screen, which made their on-screen barbs only that much more believable and funny.

I Love Lucy® made its debut on October 15, 1951, and by the end of its first season had climbed to No. 3 in the ratings. More and more people tuned in each week to see Lucy's latest misadventure or harebrained scheme to break into Ricky's act. Ball explained her character's popularity this way: "She's an exaggeration of thousands of housewives. She has always done things I feel other ladies would like to do with their husbands, their children and their bosses."

In only its second season, *I Love Lucy®* faced the prospect of stopping production when Lucy became

When viewers weren't being entertained by Lucy's talent for physical comedy, as in classic episodes involving grape-crushing in Italy (left) and a candy production line gone haywire (above), they could chuckle at the barbs exchanged by Fred and Ethel (right).

pregnant with the couple's second child. (Their first, Lucie, was born in 1951.) In a move that was considered highly controversial at the time, they decided to continue shooting and write Lucy's pregnancy into the story line. This would be the first time that a television show had dealt with the subject of pregnancy. The show's sponsor, Philip Morris Inc., initially balked at the idea but quickly backed down after Arnaz made a personal appeal to Alfred Lyons, chairman of the board of Philip Morris. CBS, however, requested that when referring to Lucy's condition the show use the word "expectant" rather than "pregnant." On January 19, 1953, some 44 million viewers tuned in to

watch the episode in which Lucy gave birth to Little Ricky. On the very same day, Lucille Ball gave birth to Desi Arnaz IV. The show drew 71.7 percent of the viewing audience, which was more than the 67.7 percent who tuned in for President Eisenhower's inauguration the following day.

During its third season, *I Love Lucy*® had to overcome an obstacle of a different and more threatening sort when Ball was called before Senator Joseph McCarthy's House Un-American Activities Committee (HUAC) to defend herself against accusations that she was a communist. It seems that years earlier, at the behest of her grandfather, she had registered as a communist prior to a local election. Although she never voted and the registration

expired after two years, because of this brief membership and her strong defense of various colleagues who had been brought before HUAC some years earlier, Ball's patriotism was called into question. She, along with Desi, strongly defended herself against these accusations and was eventually cleared by HUAC and the FBI, who deemed her early actions "politically immature." The ordeal took its emotional toll on Ball but her work on the show was as strong as ever.

In the years that followed, the Ricardos and Mertzes traveled to Hollywood, where they met up with such stars as John Wayne and Harpo Marx, and to Europe, where Lucy engaged in a classic wrestling match in a vat of grapes in Italy. In the show's final

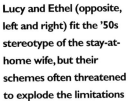
Lucy and Ethel (opposite, left and right) fit the '50s stereotype of the stay-at-home wife, but their schemes often threatened to explode the limitations of that role; Ball's home life with Arnaz and children Lucie and Desi (above) ended in divorce in 1960, but *I Love Lucy*® (above, right) remains in syndication today.

season, 1956–57, the Ricardos moved to Connecticut and the Mertzes soon followed. *I Love Lucy*® was still the top-rated program on TV but Lucy and Desi decided that six years of doing the show was enough. The long hours associated with producing a weekly show and the stress of running Desilu had taken its toll, especially on Desi and Lucille's marriage.

In the three years after the last episode of *I Love Lucy*®, Ball and Arnaz filmed 13 one-hour specials entitled *The Lucy-Desi Comedy Hour.* On March 3, 1960, one day after their final show, Ball filed for divorce from Arnaz, thereby ending an almost 20-year union that had produced two children, a successful production company and surely one of the funniest television shows of all time.

Aftermath

After his divorce from Ball, Desi Arnaz continued as president of Desilu, which went on to produce numerous hit TV shows such as *The Dick Van Dyke Show, The Untouchables* and *Star Trek.* He died from lung cancer on December 2, 1986.

Lucille Ball bought out Desi Arnaz's share of Desilu in 1962 and became the first woman ever to own a major film studio. She went on to star in the successful *The Lucy Show* from 1962 to 1968 and then *Here's Lucy* from 1968 to 1974. She also made several more films, including *Mame* in 1974. She made one last attempt at TV comedy with 1986's *Life with Lucy,* but the show was canceled after two months due to poor ratings. Lucille Ball died after heart surgery on April 26, 1989.

Both Lucille Ball and Desi Arnaz will be remembered not only through reruns of *I Love Lucy*®, which are still broadcast all over the world, but also for creating a half-hour situation comedy that became the blueprint for all those that followed.

MOVIES GO 3-D

The popularity of 3-D movies during the early 1950s rose as quickly as it fell. But when 3-D was hot, the enthusiasm was as real as the blue and red lenses in the cardboard frames that teetered on the noses of audience members.

The meteoric rise of this quintessential fad perhaps can be traced to the culture of the 1950s and to the American appetite for advanced technology, especially in entertainment. The public was evolving into a population of malleable consumers who bought any product deemed new, whether it was pastel-colored kitchen appliances or tickets for a movie promising that monsters would seem to step off the screen, or stars like Ann Miller would appear to be dancing down the aisles.

In technical terms, 3-D is known as stereoscopy, although it's doubtful the average person spoke of the medium as such. Stereoscopic filmmaking in the United States dates back to the second decade of the twentieth century. While a few 3-D features were made in the 1920s, the Hollywood studios generally were not interested in producing them, and the development of the genre fell largely to amateurs.

By 1952 television had cut movie-house audiences in half and industry moguls were looking for a way to woo viewers back. They hoped, at least for a time, that 3-D was the answer. Each studio acquired its own 3-D provider in the early '50s. The process of making images appear to reach out to the audience was relatively simple. Two projectors at the back of the theater simultaneously cast a pair of overlapping images onto the movie screen. The audience wore polarized lenses so that they could see the dual images as one.

The first "deepie," as the films were called, in a reference to their illusory visual depth, to become a hit was the African adventure story *The Lions of Gulu,* starring Robert Stack (more

Movie audiences (left and above) found the in-your-face 3-D effects captivating—at least at first.

"They'll wear toilet seats around their necks if you give 'em what they want to see!"

—BILL THOMAS, *Paramount Pictures executive, on the contention that people would not wear 3-D glasses.*

recently of the television series *Unsolved Mysteries*). Released in late November 1952 and later renamed *Bwana Devil*, it became a top-grossing film and ascended into accepted Hollywood history as the first 3-D feature. Enticing the public with the new cinematic trick, an advertisement for the film shouted, THE FLAT SCREEN IS GONE! YOU—NOT A CAMERA—BUT YOU ARE THERE! *Bwana Devil*'s first week's gross of $95,000 broke box-office records despite a consensus among critics that the script was awful. Still, audiences loved the optical illusion of man-eating lions leaping right out of the screen.

The 3-D boom was in full swing by the spring of 1953, apparently unaffected by technical glitches in the presentation of the films, such as screens that were too dark, ghosted images and bad sound. Plots, too, were less than stellar. Apparently regarding these major lapses as mere peccadilloes, audiences kept going back, even to see such grim fare as a medical documentary on a stomach operation.

Decidedly more entertaining was Warner Bros.' *House of Wax*, starring Vincent Price as Professor Henry Jarrod, the mad sculptor who plunged his murder victims into hot wax to create museum dis-

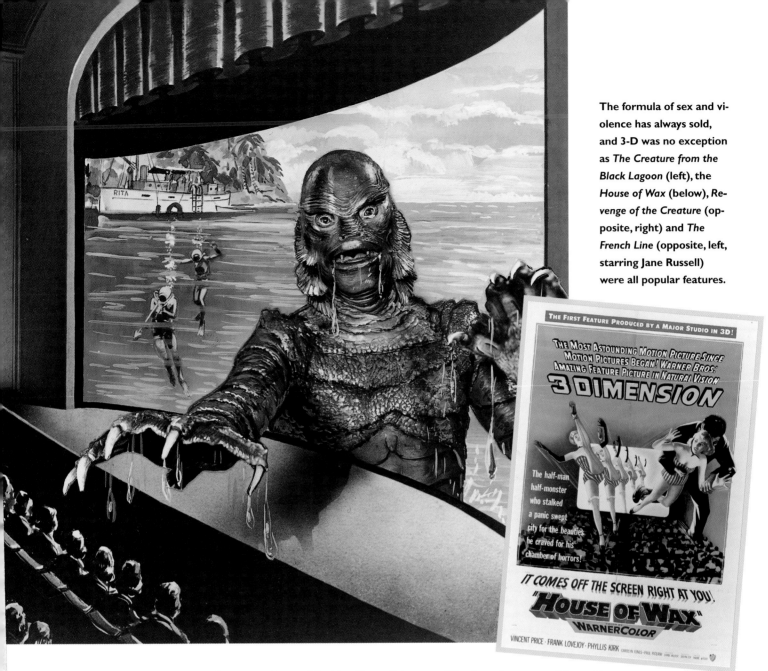

THE FIRST FEATURE PRODUCED BY A MAJOR STUDIO IN 3D!

THE MOST ASTOUNDING MOTION PICTURE SINCE MOTION PICTURES BEGAN! WARNER BROS.' AMAZING FEATURE PICTURE IN NATURAL VISION

3 DIMENSION

The half-man half-monster who stalked a panic swept city for the beauties he craved for his chamber of horrors!

IT COMES OFF THE SCREEN RIGHT AT YOU!
"HOUSE OF WAX" WARNERCOLOR

VINCENT PRICE · FRANK LOVEJOY · PHYLLIS KIRK

plays. It melted box-office records worldwide. In addition to superior color quality and true surround sound, the film featured a young Charles Bronson, then Charles Buchinsky, as Igor, the professor's mute assistant.

The success of *House of Wax* aside, 3-D film-makers often missed the mark when it came to fantastic story lines. Take the plotless *Cat-Women of the Moon,* in which the "Hollywood Cover Girls" donned unconvincing cat suits and attempted to create the illusion of claws by simply stiffening their fingers. But while audiences failed to suspend disbelief while viewing the hokey *Cat-Women,* they

did so willingly when watching *Creature from the Black Lagoon.* Widely seen as one of the greatest monster movies ever made, the film features the Creature, a.k.a the Gill-Man, who remains one of Hollywood's most popular fiends.

Moviegoers were also intrigued by 3-D Westerns like the *Charge at Feather River,* starring Guy Madison, TV's Wild Bill Hickok. Released in the summer of 1953, it was one of the year's 25 top-grossing films. The low-budget Western wowed young viewers, but suffers mightily when compared with today's cinematic achievements.

Even the Three Stooges got into the act with

The popularity of 3-D extended to Westerns (above) and animated features (left); the fad even had a print spinoff, Three Dimension Comics (opposite), in which images seemed to leap off the printed page at rapt readers.

Pardon My Backfire and *Spooks*, both released in August 1953. The films lasted a scant 16 minutes each but were loaded with laughs and 3-D tricks.

The novelty of 3-D could only last so long though. Once audiences began to tire of the technical wizardry, they were left with nothing but weak plots, tired tricks and mechanical shortcomings—hardly the stuff of box-office draws. By October 1953, productions of 3-D films slowed, with the exception of small-scale ventures like the cartoons *Popeye—The Ace of Space,* and Woody Woodpecker's *Hypnotic Hick.*

Among the last successful feature-length deepies

to be released was Metro-Goldwyn-Mayer's *Kiss Me Kate*. Starring Kathryn Grayson, Howard Keel and Ann Miller, it was billed as "Hollywood's First Important Big Musical in 3-D." Audiences agreed, and the 3-D version of the musical comedy outsold the "flat" version. John Wayne's Western, *Hondo*, which was released the next day, was so successful that the press thought a 3-D revival was afoot. Such predictions were based more on hype than fact. And so went 3-D movies, prosperous at the box office in the early 1950s, box-office poison ever after. The glasses, however, remain a popular item among movie-memoribilia collectors.

Aftermath

Although 3-D movies have never regained the popularity they enjoyed in the early 1950s, production of 3-D films continued, haltingly, over the subsequent years. Notable titles include Andy Warhol's *Flesh for Frankenstein* (1974), *Friday the 13th—Part III* (1982), and *Jaws 3-D* (1983).

Attempts at 3-D television have been largely unsuccessful, although Coca-Cola did produce a 3-D commercial in 1989.

KOREAN WAR

Studded with land mines and guarded by some two million soldiers, the border between South Korea and North Korea, the 38th parallel, is the most heavily armed in the world, and an ongoing reminder of a conflict that most Americans know little about, save what they have gleaned from the television program *M*A*S*H*.

Needless to say, the Korean War had little to do with the high jinks of Corporal Klinger and Radar O'Reilly. Some two million South Koreans and approximately 35,000 U.S. servicemen were killed in the three-year conflict, whose roots stretch to the beginning of the twentieth century, when Japan, after defeating Russia in Manchuria, claimed Korea as a colony.

Japan held the mountainous peninsula for four decades, until the end of World War II, when the United States and the Soviet Union divided the nation roughly in half, along the 38th parallel.

This arbitrary division was made without input from the Korean people, the matter having been settled before Korea had even got word of Japan's emperor Hirohito's surrender. American forces occupied the South while the Soviet army assumed control of the North.

By the end of 1949 both the United States and the Soviet Union had withdrawn their troops from Korea, but each side left advisers and weaponry behind. A communist government, led by Kim Il Sung, ran the North, and an ostensibly democratic one, led by the conservative president Syngman Rhee, who had been installed by the Americans, held sway in the South.

All of Asia was rapidly transforming in these early years of the Cold War, and Americans were largely unconcerned with the Korean peninsula. Secretary of State Dean Acheson made a speech in January 1950 enumerating the regions the United States would vigorously defend from communist

The three-year conflict made refugees (left) of thousands of Koreans and reduced many of their homes to rubble (above).

"The war in Korea has almost destroyed that nation.
I have never seen such devastation. I have seen, I guess,
as much blood and disaster as any living man, and
[this] just curdled my stomach.... If you go on
indefinitely, you are perpetuating a slaughter such as I
have never heard of in the history of mankind."

—*GENERAL DOUGLAS MACARTHUR,*
to Congress, following his removal as head of the Allied forces on April 11, 1951.

The daring landing at Inchon (opposite), conceived and executed by the headstrong MacArthur (above, seated) was critical to the recapturing of South Korea by the Allies; servicemen in Korea endured a punishing combination of intense heat in summer and freezing cold in winter (top, right).

aggression. Korea, along with Taiwan, was not mentioned. Perhaps emboldened by this omission, North Korea's Kim approached Soviet premier Josef Stalin in April 1950 with a plan to invade the South. Kim claimed that communist sympathizers in the South would rally around the invasion, and that he could overrun the country in three days. The United States, Kim argued, would not have time to mobilize a response, and was in any event unlikely to do so. Once assured that Red China would support the invasion, Stalin gave his assent.

On June 25, 1950, Soviet-backed North Korean forces stormed across the 38th parallel, catching the South Koreans and the Americans unprepared, and advanced upon Seoul. Presented with its first international crisis, the nascent United Nations acted quickly. U.S. president Harry Truman urged an immediate military response, and in a unanimous vote, the Security Council agreed with him. The aggressors had been so confident of the West's inaction that the Soviet envoy to the Security Council, who could h a v e vetoed

the response, did not even show up to vote.

United States general Douglas MacArthur was given command of the U.N. forces, which were predominantly South Korean and American, but also included troops from 16 other nations. For two months they were forced to retreat from the border, establishing a stronghold in the southwestern portion of the peninsula. In September MacArthur's forces counterattacked with a daring amphibious assault on the port city of Inchon and then started a sweeping northward advance. By October the North Koreans had been driven out of Seoul and back over the 38th parallel. The Allies captured the North Korean capital, Pyongyang, and drove on farther into the North, toward the Yalu River and the Chinese border.

Much to MacArthur's surprise, thousands of Chinese troops flooded across that border in November to aid the North Koreans. The Allies were routed and pushed back across the 38th parallel. MacArthur favored attacking China, preferably with nuclear weapons, and said so loudly. Truman believed any engagement on Chinese soil would provoke the Soviet Union and trigger a third world war. MacArthur persisted, and Truman eventually replaced him with General Matthew Ridgway.

The war stalemated, and negotiations to end it began in June 1951. Still the fighting ground on for more than two years. Horribly bloody but indecisive battles raged in the mountains, which U.S. troops gave nicknames like Heartbreak Ridge and Porkchop Hill. Finally, on July 27, 1953, an armistice was reached. Though everyone involved had complaints about the settlement, the West had sent an unambiguous message about its resolve in the face of communist aggression. And the Cold War positions adopted by the United States and the Soviet Union were drawn hard and fast along the tensely guarded 38th parallel.

Aftermath

Inconclusive though it was, the Korean conflict served to heighten U.S. concern over communist expansion in Asia, and resulted in a major buildup in the U.S. defense budget. Truman increased aid to the French in Indochina, a policy continued by the Eisenhower and Kennedy administrations that led to U.S. involvement in the Vietnam War, another bloody conflict in Asia that would last until 1975.

North Korea's Kim Il Sung proved remarkably durable, ruling the country until his death in 1994, when his son, Kim Jong Il, assumed control. In the mid-'90s North Korea was plagued by flood, drought, economic hardship and starvation. Its relations with the United States remain tense, as underscored by North Korea's 1998 saber-rattling over U.S. attempts to inspect its suspected nuclear weapons production sites.

U.S. soldiers had an extensive taste of jungle warfare (opposite) in Korea, a mode of combat that would be repeated in Vietnam; while U.S. GIs enjoyed happy homecomings (top, right), Koreans were left with a nation in ruins (above).

ROCKY MARCIANO

Perfection in sports is a difficult goal. A critical fumble, a bad bounce in the infield, a lucky punch—any number of factors can bring a would-be perfectionist back to reality in an instant. And so it is that the world of sports has always had a special place in its pantheon for Rocky Marciano, the hardworking son of a humble shoemaker who retired from boxing as the only undefeated champion in heavyweight history.

Born in 1923 in the predominantly Irish and Italian working-class town of Brockton, Massachusetts, Marciano was the eldest of six children struggling to survive during the Great Depression. As a boy Marciano participated in a variety of sports including boxing, wrestling and baseball, which was his favorite. In fact, his love of baseball later led him to an unsuccessful tryout with the North Carolina-based farm club of the Chicago Cubs.

When he was drafted into the army in 1943,

Marciano began to realize his potential as a boxer in bouts with other enlisted men. After his discharge in 1946, he wrote to Madison Square Garden, the boxing Mecca of New York, and requested a professional trial. Most observers, including trainer Joe Cirelli, who had seen Marciano fight, believed he was wasting his time. Cirelli told him, "You're too old to be starting out. You're not tall enough. Your arms are too short and your legs are too thick. Forget boxing. You'd get killed in the pros."

Such pessimistic predictions notwithstanding, Marciano was granted his pro trial in New York, where he was seen by manager Al Weill, who organized matches for the International Boxing Club at Madison Square Garden. Weill was decidedly underwhelmed by Marciano at first, but, seeing an opportunity to promote the raw 5-foot 10-inch, 190-pound fighter as a "Great White

Marciano (left, and with wife Barbara, above) was the only undefeated heavyweight champion in history.

Hope," he eventually hooked him up with 60-year-old British trainer Charley Goldman. Noting Marciano's short stature and limited reach, Goldman would help him develop the signature crouching style that made Marciano elusive while at the same time providing him with a solid base from which to launch his lunging, swarming forays. This idiosyncratic method, combined with Marciano's devastating punching power, made him extremely effective.

Marciano turned pro on March 17, 1947, fighting unimpressively under the name "Rocky Mack." Sixteen months later, under Goldman's tutelage, and using his real name, Marciano scored a first-round knockout of Harry Bilazarian. He fought 10 more times that year and won all 10 bouts by KO. After

racking up 35 straight victories, Marciano got his first major fight in 1951 against highly regarded and hard-hitting Rex Layne. From his characteristic crouch, Marciano worked over the outside of Layne's arms and body with a barrage of hooks, a strategy that became his trademark. By the sixth round Layne, who could barely raise his arms to defend himself, was an easy target for Marciano's knockout punch. That same year Marciano defeated his boyhood idol, Joe Louis, who was in the midst of

"No one ever accused Rocky Marciano of being a good boxer, but with his power, he didn't have to be."

—DON DUNPHY, *ring announcer*

a comeback attempt. A battered Louis went down for good in the eighth round, ending his comeback bid and reducing Marciano to tears.

With these impressive victories, Marciano was ready for a title shot. Champion Jersey Joe Walcott gave the young bull his opportunity in 1952. Few observers thought Marciano had much of a chance against the savvy Walcott, and when a Walcott left hook sent him to the canvas in the opening round, it seemed they were right. But Marciano got up quickly, then nailed Walcott with a vicious right when the champion tried to move in and finish him off. In Rounds 2 through 12 Marciano relentlessly pursued Walcott around the ring, absorbing punishment from all conceivable angles, until he finally caught up with the tiring champion in the

13th round. Behind on points, Marciano delivered a solid right to Walcott's jaw that knocked him unconscious and transformed the shoemaker's son into the heavyweight champion of the world.

During his reign as heavyweight champ, the man who would come to be known as "The Brockton Blockbuster" gained enormous respect for his ability to absorb blows and dish them out with his sledgehammer right, once described by sportswriter Red Smith as "a right hand that registered nine on the Richter scale." He defended his title six times in a three-year span from 1952 to '55.

In his final defense, against 38-year-old Archie Moore in 1955, Marciano once again recovered from an early knockdown; this time he caught up with his opponent and knocked

him senseless in the ninth round. The Moore fight—as well as a string of previous tough bouts, including two against former champ Ezzard Charles in 1954—helped convince Marciano that it was time to retire. Two other factors that surely influenced his decision were his growing distaste for manager Weill, who was getting what Marciano considered an unfairly large percentage of his purses, and his wife, Barbara, who had simply seen enough boxing brutality inflicted upon her husband. Finally, there was the instructive example of Louis, who had diminished his otherwise sterling boxing legacy by fighting on too long. And so in April 1956, at the age of 32 and to the shock of the boxing establishment, Rocky Marciano announced his retirement from the ring. His formidable, and to this day unequaled, record of 49 wins (43 by knockout) without a defeat remains one of the sport's most impressive achievements.

Marciano walked away from boxing and, unlike too many others in boxing and sports in general, never looked back. He retired to Fort Lauderdale, Florida, with Barbara, daughter Mary Anne and adopted son Rocky Jr. But even in retirement Marciano kept busy with public appearances, speaking engagements and occasional work as a boxing commentator.

Rocky Marciano died in a plane crash en route to one of his appearances on August 31, 1969, just one day shy of his 46th birthday. His legacy of perfection remains untouched.

A Marciano miscellany: knocking Roland LaStarza through the ropes in 1953 (opposite, above); posing with the St. Patrick's baseball team in Brockton in 1940 (left, back row, second from left); celebrating with a few of his legion of young fans in New York (below, left); and undergoing an exam by his father Peter (below).

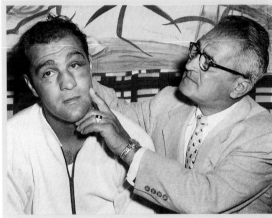

Aftermath

It has been three decades since Rocky Marciano's untimely death, but he remains a popular American icon. His story unquestionably influenced Sylvester Stallone's Academy Award-winning movie, *Rocky,* and today's heavyweights still pursue his undefeated record and study his fights.

In September 1985, Larry Holmes was on the brink of tying Marciano's record of 49 consecutive wins without a defeat when he lost a close 15-round decision to Michael Spinks, leaving him with a record of 48–1. No one has approached Rocky Marciano's mark since.

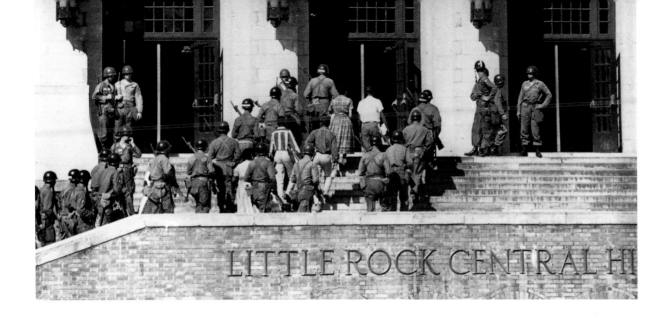

PUBLIC SCHOOL DESEGREGATION

Our Constitution is color-blind, and neither knows nor tolerates classes among its citizens. In respect of civil rights, all citizens are equal before the law.

So wrote Justice John Marshall Harlan as the sole dissenting voice in the Supreme Court's portentous and flawed 1896 ruling on *Plessy v. Ferguson*. The decision declared that as long as separate but equal facilities were provided for blacks and whites, segregation did not violate the Constitution. It set the country on a 60-year course of legal (de jure) segregation and made a mockery of the Constitution. By the end of the nineteenth century, the Supreme Court had stripped African-Americans of the rights granted them by the Fourteenth and Fifteenth Amendments in the post-Civil War Reconstruction years: Their right to equal protection under the law and their right to vote were gone.

Largely illiterate and politically, legally, and economically disenfranchised, blacks were severely restricted by a variety of Jim Crow policies. In cities across the South, buses, restrooms, movie houses, barbershops, swimming pools, baseball parks and even houses of ill repute fell under the "separate but equal" doctrine of *Plessy*. Nowhere was the discrimination inherent in Jim Crow more injurious than in public school education. For if blacks were ever to achieve anything close to equal status, education would be key.

By the onset of the Depression, separate and *unequal* schools seemed to be an unassailable institution. In the rural South where segregation was most deeply entrenched, black schools routinely received only a fraction of the funds allocated to white schools. Run-down, one-room schoolhouses lacked heating and plumbing; teachers were poorly paid; buses, if they existed, were old and prone to break down; and classrooms were sorely overcrowded. Blacks fared better in the North, but many who had migrated for jobs during

It took federal troops (above) to protect Elizabeth Eckford (left) and the other black students in Little Rock from angry mobs.

COLORED

Discriminatory Jim Crow practices included separate drinking fountains (inset) and classrooms (above) as well as requirements that blacks ride in the back of public buses (opposite); in 1955 Rosa Parks (opposite, far right) refused to do so and her subsequent arrest and court case led to the outlawing of discrimination in public transportation.

and after World War I found themselves in a system of de facto segregation caused by discriminatory housing patterns that forced blacks into the ghettos.

Far too little had changed when, on May 17, 1954, the landmark Supreme Court decision on *Brown v. the Board of Education of Topeka, Kansas*—

actually five separate cases grouped as one—finally declared segregated schools inherently discriminatory and blew asunder *Plessy v. Ferguson*.

The legal battle had been raging for two decades. Brilliant and dedicated black lawyers like Charles Houston, William Hastie and Thurgood Marshall had slowly and skillfully whittled away at racist legal precedents in education, beginning with graduate schools, the integration of which they reasoned would cause far less alarm to whites than the integration of elemen-

"In these days, it is doubtful that any child may reasonably be expected to succeed in life if he is denied the opportunity of an education."

—*CHIEF JUSTICE EARL WARREN, May 17, 1954*

tary and high schools. Usually under the banner of the National Association for the Advancement of Colored People (NAACP), they fought from the lower courts up until the right to equal, if separate, facilities was beyond argument. Then, encouraged by progress blacks had made during World War II and under the leadership of Marshall, the NAACP launched a head-on challenge to the legitimacy of the separate-but-equal rule established in *Plessy*.

Even then, *Plessy* did not fall easily. After the initial hearing of *Brown*, the Supreme Court, which was badly splintered under Chief Justice Fred Vinson, stalled by ordering a reargument. In

the meantime, Eisenhower replaced Truman in the White House. And when Vinson died of a heart attack in the fall of '53, Eisenhower appointed Earl Warren, the Republican governor of California, as the new chief justice. Viewed as a moderate at the time, Warren would preside over a series of landmark decisions broadening the protections afforded to individual citizens by the Constitution and hence the right of the federal Justice Department to intervene in a variety of areas that had previously been reserved to the states. "It was the biggest damnfool mistake I ever made," said Eisenhower in later years about his appointment of Warren. A skillful mediator, Warren managed

to forge a unanimous decision on *Brown* from a court that many thought would hand down as many as nine different opinions.

But the chief justice's historic pronouncement that "separate educational facilities are inherently unequal" marked the beginning of a new battle over the implementation of the Court's decree. Virginia governor Thomas B. Stanley soon declared, "I shall use every legal means at my command to continue segregated schools," and the state of Florida proposed a labyrinthine network of hoops that blacks wishing to attend white schools would have to jump through. While some schools integrated voluntarily and without incident, many more prepared to fight tooth and nail to preserve the system the country's highest court had just declared illegal. On May 31, 1955, the Court delivered a second unanimous decision, regarding implementation of *Brown*. Unfortunately, its language was vague,

mandating only that states begin admitting students on a nondiscriminatory basis "with all deliberate speed," a standard that left the door wide open for resistance.

The single most stunning act of defiance belonged to Governor Orval Faubus of Arkansas who, on September 4, 1957, used National Guardsmen to prevent nine black students from entering Little Rock's Central High School. Three weeks later, after the growing white mob outside the school had turned violent, Eisenhower reluctantly dispatched the 101st Airborne Division. It was the first use of U.S. troops to protect the civil rights of African-Americans since Reconstruction. The Constitution may well have been color-blind, but in Little Rock that fall, it took 1,000 soldiers to open the doors for nine black schoolchildren. A seminal legal victory had been won, but the war that was supposed to have ended in 1865 clearly was still being fought.

Marshall (left, second from right) led the NAACP's legal team as it entered the Supreme Court Building in December 1952; the first black students in Little Rock not only needed federal protection to enter school but also required an armed escort upon leaving (opposite).

Aftermath

A decade after *Brown,* only 1.17 percent of black children in the South were in schools with whites, a by-product of ever-increasing de facto segregation due to white flight and efforts by urban officials to subvert the intention of *Brown* by creating segregated school districts. Marshall, who became the first black Supreme Court justice in 1967, dissented in a 1974 case that ruled against municipally engineered integration: "Our nation, I fear, will be ill-served by the Court's refusal to remedy separate and unequal education, for unless our children begin to learn together, there is little hope that our people will ever learn to live together." One place where black and white children do learn together today is Little Rock's racially balanced Central High School, which was named a national historic site by President Clinton in 1998.

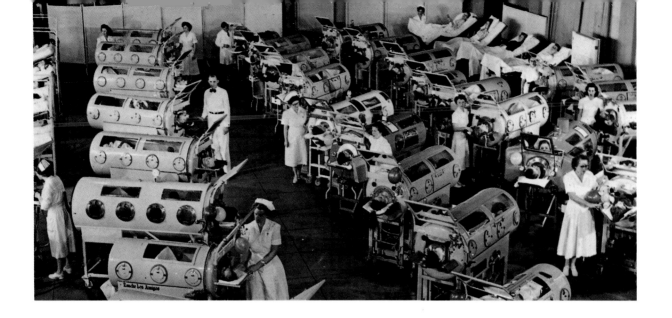

POLIO VACCINE DEVELOPED

Anxious parents forbade children to seek relief from the sweltering heat in swimming pools. They told them to stay away from air-conditioned movie houses. They warned them to avoid crowds and drinking fountains. These were not the strictures of paranoid, overprotective parents; families were properly concerned, lest the menacing shadow of "the Crippler" as paralytic poliomyelitis, or polio, was familiarly called, fall across them. It was the summer of 1952 and the country was in the throes of its worst epidemic of infantile paralysis ever. Nearly 58,000 cases were reported by year's end; more than 3,000 of them were fatal. Most of those who survived faced years of rehabilitation followed by lives with withered limbs, in iron lungs, wheelchairs or cumbersome leg braces.

An Egyptian stele depicts a victim of polio as early as 1500 B.C. Ironically, it wasn't until improvements in public hygiene lowered immunities that polio transformed into an epidemic disease seen mostly in developed countries, especially in summer. During the first half of the twentieth century, waves of polio infected thousands annually in the United States—killing some and crippling others.

Without doubt the most famous polio survivor was Franklin Delano Roosevelt, who escaped the terrible epidemic of 1916 in New York but contracted the disease in 1921.

Although as president FDR concealed his disability from the public—photographs of him in a wheelchair are very rare—it is fair to say he changed the course of polio history through the publicity and the funding he brought to the fight against disease. At the time of FDR's election to the presidency in 1932, most virologists and epidemiologists searching for a polio vaccine were operating under seriously flawed assumptions. Five years later Roosevelt formed the National Foundation for Infantile Paralysis and asked his friend, adviser and fellow polio crusader

Salk and his vaccine (left) saved hundreds of thousands of children from confinement in iron lungs (above).

 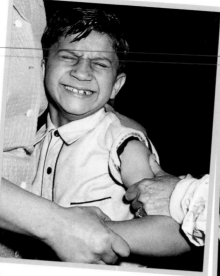 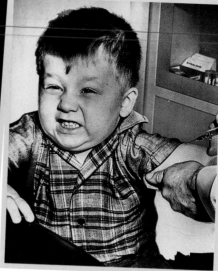

Basil O'Connor to head it. FDR wanted the Foundation to "lead, direct and unify the fight on every phase of this sickness."

After Roosevelt's death in 1945, O'Connor, who had become frustrated with the volunteer organization's lack of progress in scientific research, appointed Dr. Harry Weaver as director of research to get things moving. Weaver quickly established a polio typing program to determine if there were more than the three distinct types of poliovirus that had already been identified, a necessary, if monotonous, step in the march toward a vaccine. A young virologist named Jonas Salk emerged as the program's driving force.

When Salk learned in 1948 that the polio virus could be grown in nonnervous tissue cultures—a Nobel Prize-winning breakthrough by Harvard researchers John Enders, Thomas Weller and Frederick Robbins—he saw the road to a vaccine. Influenced by his previous work on an influenza vaccine, and backed by O'Connor, Salk began working on a so-called killed-virus vaccine rather than the more generally favored live-virus vaccine. "Dogma held that you couldn't immunize with a killed virus; you had to go through an infection to get immunity," Salk said years later.

The ordeal of getting vaccinated (above and opposite) against the polio virus became a rite of passage for millions of children in the '50s, one that was endured with varying degrees of stoicism.

By the spring of 1952, Salk was ready to test his "Formalin-inactivated poliovirus preparations" (as he called the early vaccine) on a group of polio patients. The shots produced more antibodies in the patients than the disease itself had and caused no ill effects. More inoculations were conducted with equal success. When the results were announced to the Foundation's immunization committee in early 1953, many on the committee argued against rushing into a field trial; failure could have discredited the organization and derailed further research. Even Salk favored caution. On the other hand, the country had just experienced its worst polio epidemic ever and another polio season would likely produce thousands more cases.

Word of the possible vaccine leaked out, however, and hopes around the country soared. Salk went on national radio to explain that the vaccine could not be mass tested in time for the 1953 polio

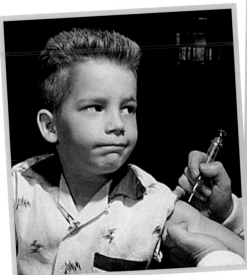

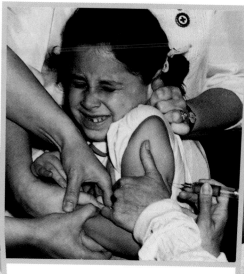

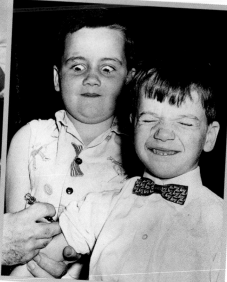

"What nearly everyone who grew up in the polio years or was raising a child then remembers was the fear that hung like heat in the summer air."

—*KATHRYN BLACK, author of* In the Shadow of Polio

season. Thirteen months later, on April 26, 1954, the largest field trial in medical history got under way, funded by the millions of dimes that had been flowing into the Foundation since entertainer Eddie Cantor had come up with the fund-raising idea called the March of Dimes in the late '30s.

More than 1.8 million school-age baby boomers, dubbed Polio Pioneers, participated in the North American trial. On April 12, 1955, the 10th anniversary of FDR's death, the vaccine was pronounced "safe, effective and potent." Church bells rang out across the country, and Salk's name became a household word. "There was suddenly a release from this great fear—the dread that occurred each summer," as Salk put it. Within weeks, thousands were lining up for shots and the annual number of cases in the United States eventually dropped to a dozen or fewer. Summertime once again belonged to children.

Aftermath

Salk's vaccine prevented an estimated 300,000 cases of polio in the six years before it was largely replaced in the United States by Albert Sabin's live-virus vaccine. In 1994, the Pan American Health Organization declared the Western Hemisphere entirely free of polio. The next year, on June 23, Jonas Salk died at age 80 in La Jolla, California. The day before his death, he was working on an AIDS vaccine at the Salk Institute in La Jolla.

While the "wild" polio virus no longer exists in the Americas, about six cases per year of "vaccine-associated paralytic polio," from the live vaccine, still occur in the United States. Because of its lack of risk, the Salk killed-virus vaccine is currently regaining popularity.

WORLD SERIES RIVALS

Imagine if Mark McGwire, Ken Griffey Jr. and Sammy Sosa each led a baseball team in the same city. In the 1950s, New York fans were blessed with an equivalent embarrassment of riches, as Gotham was home to three Hall of Fame center fielders: Mickey Mantle for the Yankees, Willie Mays for the Giants and Duke Snider for the Dodgers. And the list of stars didn't end there. The New York City talent pool was deeper than center field at the Polo Grounds. Jackie Robinson, Whitey Ford, Pee Wee Reese, Roy Campanella, Yogi Berra, Gil Hodges—these were the ballplayers who made the national pastime, in the words of writer Roger Angell, "almost a private possession of New York City" during the decade.

The Big Apple placed at least one and more often two teams in the World Series every year from

1949 to 1958. The Giants went twice, the Dodgers made it five times and the incomparable Yankees appeared in nine, winning seven. These interborough clashes became known as "subway series," and the rivalries attending them were fierce, none more so than the one between the New York Yankees and the long-suffering Brooklyn Dodgers.

For Brooklyn, the decade began with heartbreak and ended in betrayal. In 1951 the Giants' Bobby Thomson broke hearts from Bed-Stuy to Bay Ridge with his Shot Heard 'Round the World (page 22), and in '58 owner Walter O'Malley committed the unforgivable act of moving the beloved Dodgers to Los Angeles. The years in between were a catalog of crushed hopes, mitigated by one shining moment.

In '52 the Dodgers dispatched the Giants early—no miracle this year—and won the NL

By 1953 Yankees fans (opposite) were taunting Dodger fans (above) with Brooklyn's annual cry of "Wait till next year."

Major League Baseball trademarks and copyrights are used with permission of Major League Baseball Properties, Inc.

going away. The Dodgers and their fans, who had fallen to the Yankees in the 1947 and '49 World Series had a saying: "Wait till next year." But when they took a 3–2 Series edge over the Yankees with Games 6 and 7 scheduled for Ebbets Field, it seemed that next year had finally arrived. Snider belted two home runs in Game 6, but the Yankees, powered by a Mantle blast in the eighth inning, won 3–2. Mantle parked another one to win Game 7, and the Series, for the Yanks. Wait till next year, came the cry from Flatbush.

Sure enough, both teams returned to the championship in '53. This time the Dodgers were brimming with confidence. They had won a club-record 105 regular-season games. Their team batting average was .285. Snider had batted .336 with 42 home runs; Campanella, Brooklyn's talented catcher, had belted 41. Alas, another superb Brooklyn season went up in smoke as the Yankees took the Series in six games to win a record fifth straight title. Berra and Yankee second baseman Billy Martin batted .429 and .500, respectively, in the Series.

When the Dodgers and Yankees met yet again in the 1955 Series, many expected more of the same, and indeed the Yankees won the first two Series games in Yankee Stadium. But the Dodgers

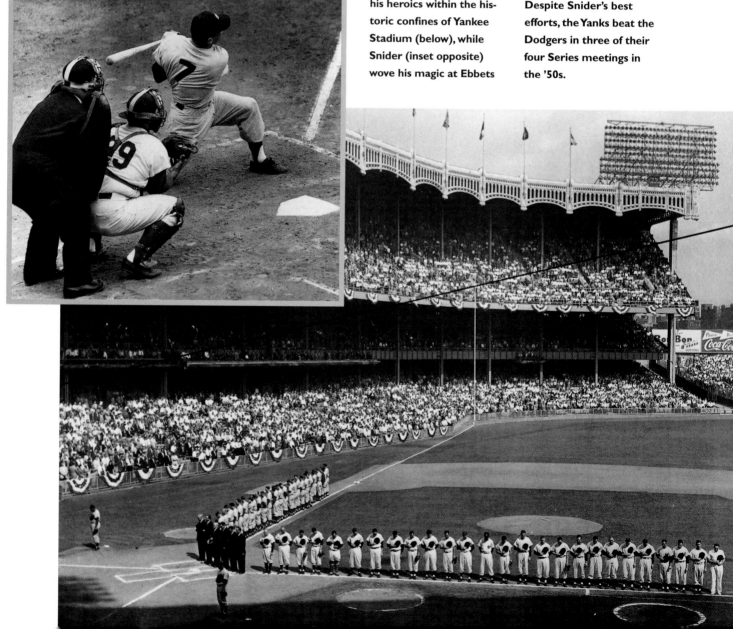

Mantle (inset) performed his heroics within the historic confines of Yankee Stadium (below), while Snider (inset opposite) wove his magic at Ebbets **Field (opposite, below). Despite Snider's best efforts, the Yanks beat the Dodgers in three of their four Series meetings in the '50s.**

"Please don't interrupt, because you haven't heard this one before ... honest. At precisely 4:45 p.m. today, in Yankee Stadium, off came the 52-year slur on the ability of the Dodgers to win a World Series, for at that moment the last straining Yankee was out at first base, and the day, the game, and the 1955 Series belonged to Brooklyn."

—SHIRLEY POVICH,
The Washington Post, *October 4, 1955*

The Yankees celebrated their fourth consecutive World Series title in 1952 (above); Hank Bauer, Berra, Martin and Joe Collins (inset, left to right) whooped it up after their fifth in '53; at the end of the '55 Series, the delirious Dodgers mobbed Podres (opposite, above), who later received congratulatory kisses from Hodges and Carl Furillo (inset opposite, left and right, respectively).

won three straight in Ebbets Field and, after dropping Game 6, wrapped up the Series with a stirring 2–0 win in Game 7. The highlights of the dramatic victory were the clutch pitching of unsung Johnny Podres, who pitched a complete-game shutout, and a spectacular running catch by diminutive Cuban outfielder Sandy Amoros, who hauled in a long fly ball down the left-field line in the sixth inning, then whirled and fired to Pee Wee Reese, who in turn fired to first to double up Gil McDougald and effectively end the only serious Yankee threat. Brooklyn had won its first, and, as it turned out, last World Series title. Tele-

phone circuits between the boroughs overloaded that night, and collapsed. The sky lit up with fireworks, and the streets filled with revelers, leaning out of their cars and on their horns. THIS IS NEXT YEAR, crowed the headline in the morning paper.

After five World Series meetings with the Yankees in nine years, the Dodgers had only one victory to show for it, but how sweet that victory was. The following year the teams returned to the World Series yet again, and the natural order of things was restored as the Dodgers won the first two games only to collapse in seven. The Yankees' Don Larsen ensured that this last subway series

Aftermath

The departure of the Dodgers and the Giants for California eliminated the possibility of a subway series until 1962, when the Mets debuted in New York. Though the Mets have since won championships, there hasn't been a subway series since '56.

Left temporarily alone in the Big Apple, the Yankees continued to win. They went to five straight Fall Classics from 1960 to '64, winning two. They won two titles in the 1970s and two—and counting—in the '90s, giving them 24 championships, more than twice the total titles of any other major league team.

O'Malley had sought greener pastures by moving his team to L.A., and he found them: In 1998 his son Peter sold the Dodgers to Australian mogul Rupert Murdoch for a reported $311 million.

would be unforgettable: He pitched a perfect game in Game 5, the only one in World Series history.

It was the last hurrah for the Golden Age of New York baseball. By decade's end both the Giants and Dodgers had moved to San Franciso and Los Angeles, respectively, sad tidings indeed for the intensely loyal fans of those two storied franchises. To add insult to injury, Ebbets Field was demolished almost immediately and the Polo Grounds fell to the wrecking ball in 1964, a pair of grievous blows that left local fans even more disillusioned about the state of their beloved game. New York baseball would never be the same.

DRIVE-IN MOVIES

Whether it provided the opportunity for a first kiss or an evening away from the folks, Saturday night at the Starlite, Star-Vue or Hi-Way Drive-in with the top down, the stars above and a schlocky monster movie on the screen remains a vivid, cherished memory to those who were teenagers in the 1950s.

The first drive-in theater, a gift from a son to his mother, was built in Camden, New Jersey, in 1933. The son, businessman Richard M. Hollingshead, had been challenged by his mother to devise a way for her to see movies without having to squeeze her robust frame into the narrow seats of the local theater. On June 6, after months of backyard experimentation, Hollingshead granted his mother's wish by opening the Camden Automobile Movie Theater. An audience of 600 people paid 25 cents each (no more than a dollar for each carload) to see *Wife Beware* starring Adolphe Menjou.

Although drive-ins soon began to appear across the country, near small towns and in rural areas, true popularity eluded the medium until the late 1940s when postwar prosperity fueled America's love for the automobile. Entrepreneurs took full advantage: Souvenir shops, gas stations and drive-in restaurants peppered the now well-traveled roads. The most popular new roadside attraction, however, was the drive-in movie theater.

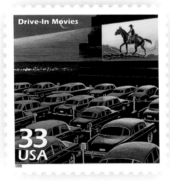

Families, not teenagers, made up most of the clientele at the early drive-ins. They would arrive long before showtime to picnic against a backdrop of mountains or lush foliage, show off their new automobile and socialize while playgrounds and refreshment stands kept the children happy. At sundown, the screen would come alive with such classics as *My Little Chickadee*, with W.C. Fields and Mae West, or *Ride 'em Cowboy*, starring the inimitable Abbott and Costello.

"Unlike the conventional theater, which pri-

Some went to drive-in theaters (above) for the movie, others for the enticing cover of darkness (left).

75

"In the old days, I got to the point where if I didn't see two heads and couldn't identify them both, I didn't stop and ask them if they wanted bug spray for mosquitoes, because it was the passion pit."

—*SAM KIRKLAND, owner (and former employee) of the Sky-Vue Drive-In Theater in LaMesa, Texas*

marily sells its screen attraction, drive-in theater advertising must concentrate on the full evening's inexpensive entertainment it offers to the entire family, of which movies are only a part," said Paul Petersen, a theater executive. Indeed, the back side of the screen tower often faced the highway and served as an elaborate neon- and mural-covered billboard advertising the venue as well as the current attraction. One Long Island, New York, drive-in offered 25-cent pony rides, baby parades, and talent shows between

the screen and the front row of cars. Kids loved the excitement, parents loved the convenience.

That scene changed in the 1950s. Mom and Dad took to television and made the home their entertainment hub. Teens, restless under the parental glare, longed for privacy and outings with their friends. Enter the "passion pit"—the place for young men to take their best girls and their fathers' Chevrolets. As with the drive-ins of the '40s, the movie was hardly the main attraction. The real enticement now was the privacy afforded by

Some of the drive-in theater marquees (above and opposite page) were works of art in themselves; the drive-in **speaker or squawk box (right) was introduced in 1946 and allowed viewers to adjust the volume as they saw fit.**

steamed-up car windows—a benefit that many a randy teen would sneak in through an exit or stow away in a trunk to enjoy.

The Hollywood brass, appalled by such drive-in promotions as "children under 12 admitted free," and "buck night"—in which every car, no matter how many passengers it carried, got in for only $1—did everything it could to discourage the new medium. Most damaging were the exorbitant rental fees that the studios set for their first-run features, a situation that forced most drive-ins to run mostly mediocre fare. It also didn't help that drive-in theaters were for the most part independently owned, meaning the studios made far less money exhibiting their movies on drive-in movie screens than at indoor theaters, most of which were owned by the studios. When the courts ruled that such ownership was monopolistic, the quality of drive-in films still didn't improve because the major studios continued to determine the rental price of first-run features.

A major source of revenue for drive-in owners was food, hawked on-screen with less than subtle graphics (below), sold at concession stands (above) during a break in **the film, and in some cases delivered directly to patrons by theater employees (right); outdoor concerts (opposite) offered operators a source of income during the day.**

Of course the Hollywood studios weren't the only pesky problem facing intrepid drive-in operators; they also had to deal with the persistent nuisance of bugs. Warm, starry nights, flawless as they may have been in the mind's eye, were less so in reality as young lovers were frequently attacked by legions of bloodthirsty mosquitoes. When "Car Nets" designed to fit over the frame of the driver's-side windows failed to fend off the unwanted guests, operators sprayed the chemical DDT, which was somewhat effective but produced a foul odor. Determined to alleviate the dual problem of bugs and sweltering heat, theater owners in the South experimented with underground pipes that delivered cold air into cars.

REFRESHMENT STAND

VISIT OUR Refreshment stand

Unfortunately, mice and bugs would crawl into the pipes during the day, and get blown into the cars along with the cool air at night. Moviegoers understandably preferred to sweat—and swat—it out rather than watch *I Was A Teenage Werewolf* with a car full of vermin.

In spite of such glitches, by 1958 more than 4,000 drive-ins dotted the country. Teenage boys just couldn't get enough of sitting close to their steadies, ever ready to "comfort" them at the sight of the Blob. They never knew they were creating a scene as enduring as any film ever made.

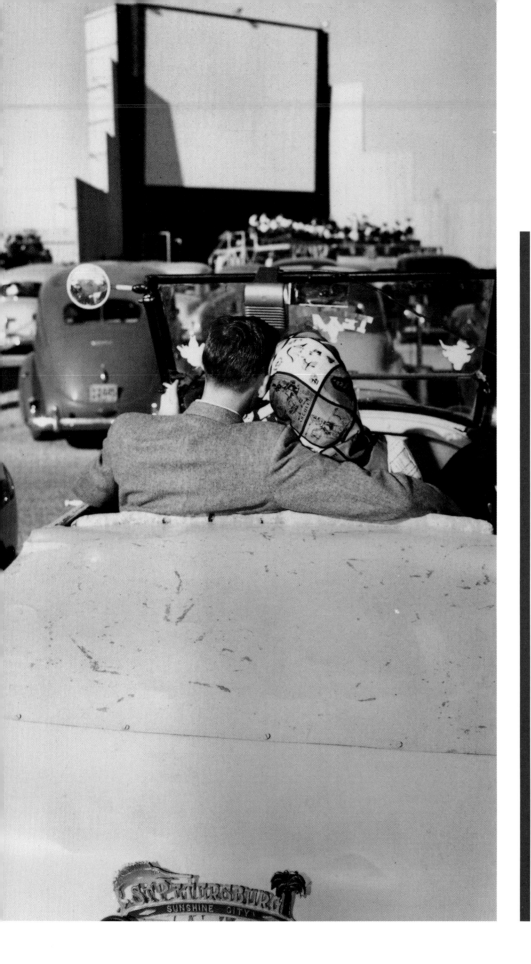

Aftermath

By the late '50s, the drive-in market was nearly saturated. The beach-blanket flicks that dominated the screens during the 1960s failed to sustain the interest of the new crop of teens, and by the close of that decade construction of new drive-ins ended. Lean economic times caused drive-in facilities to deteriorate. Leasing the lot for Saturday swap meets was one survival tactic that continues today.

The public hardly noticed the debut of radio sound in the 1970s. To boost profits, operators turned to pornographic films. Real-estate developers showed the most interest in drive-ins during the late '70s and early '80s, recognizing the sites as prime locales for shopping malls.

In the '80s, cable television, the VCR and the metamorphosis of the movie house into a multi-screened megaplex further eclipsed the drive-in. In 1997 fewer than 600 drive-in movie theaters remained in the United States.

TEEN FASHIONS

Names and dates might escape the memory bank, but the feel of a tight fuzzy sweater, the task of scuffing saddle shoes just so and the act of cuffing a favorite pair of blue jeans before meeting friends at the drive-in stay locked inside forever. Such is fashion's power, and the teenagers of the 1950s made the most of it.

No longer expected to help support the family financially, middle-class teens used income from lawn-mowing, baby-sitting and allowances to ride high on the crest of American consumerism. With an estimated $9 billion to spend, according to a 1957 *Newsweek* story, teenagers were ready, willing and able to buy just about any fashion item in sight, and this made them prime targets for marketers and media. As much as Mom and Dad wanted their sons and daughters to emulate them in their style of dress, the younger set looked instead to silver-screen idols, the "boob tube" and magazines like *Seventeen* for guidance. But if teenagers were hellbent on making a sartorial statement distinct from their parents', they were also nearly compulsive in their conformity among themselves. The large-scale availability of ready-to-wear clothing that began after World War II certainly facilitated their cookie-cutter dressing. And if there was one article of clothing that served as the cornerstone of both men's and women's fashion in the '50s, it was blue jeans.

Known first as "dungarees," denim pants underwent a gradual transformation from the "uniform" of sailors, farmers and cowboys to casual clothes for suburban fathers with lawns to mow and burgers to barbecue. The durability, washability and low cost of dungarees soon endeared them to all ages and both sexes; even Marilyn Monroe was photographed wearing them. It was teens, though, not adults, who ultimately immortalized the style.

The boys (left) emulated James Dean, the girls (above) aped Debbie Reynolds and the marketers had a field day.

Teenage girls paired untucked men's button-down shirts with jeans rolled up at the ankle to expose bobbysocks and saddle shoes. Boys, too, wore their jeans cuffed at the ankle, but if they topped them with a white T-shirt and a black leather jacket—instead of, say, a brightly colored patterned shirt—they were no longer communicating the slouchy freedom of adolescence, but rather the smoldering menace of the rebel, embodied by screen idols Marlon Brando (*The Wild One*, 1953) and James Dean (*Rebel Without a Cause* and *East of Eden*, both 1955).

Not surprisingly, the "greaser" look, with its sideburns, pompadours and Elvis-inspired attire, made guardians of moral decency jittery at first. Certain that kids who dressed like the king of rock 'n' roll were doomed to a life of depravity, high-school principals at a 1957 convention voted to ban blue jeans, ducktail haircuts and Elvis records from future dances. But the momentum was too great. Elvis-inspired black jeans with emerald green stitching and Elvis's signature stamped on the leather patch pocket had hit teen wish lists in 1956; more than 70,000 pairs of the jeans flew off the shelves before the '56 Christmas shopping season even began.

Not that denim completely dominated teen wardrobes. Females going for the girl-next-door look epitomized by Doris Day and Debbie Reynolds attended informal dances wearing full, wool-felt skirts appliquéd with bright motifs, like the ubiquitous poodle on a leash. Two or more ny-

"You can do anything, but don't step on my blue suede shoes."

—*CARL PERKINS, "Blue Suede Shoes," 1956*

Teen fashions ranged from button-down shirts and wide, belted skirts (opposite) to T-shirts and jeans or chinos (left and above, right); those on the Kerouac beat tended toward rougher fabrics and, of course, the mandatory beard (above, left).

lon petticoats rustled underneath these voluminous skirts. Girls would dip the petticoats in a sugar solution and then drip-dry them for maximum stiffness and the fullest, most stylish look, not to mention wonderful undulations during spins around the dance floor. They topped the fluffy skirts with tightfitting Peter Pan-collared blouses, and cinched their waists with wide belts. The waist-hip contrast flourished until 1957, when loose-fitting styles, particularly the sack dress or chemise, emigrated from France.

For sipping milk shakes at a diner with a date,

that same girl-next-door aspirant might pair a pencil-slim skirt with a sweater trimmed with decorative beads. As for her hair, if it wasn't a pixie or a pageboy, it was either secured in a high ponytail accented with a colorful scarf, or cropped short with curls close to the head in a poodle cut. Saddle shoes, loafers or other flat footwear accompanied either skirt style. High heels were worn only by mothers, socialites and fashion models.

More casual pastimes, such as bicycling or lying

on the floor chatting on the phone, called for figure-hugging, calf-length pedal pushers, such as the ones worn by Shirley Jones in the 1957 film *April Love*. Pedal pushers, or capri pants, usually had the zipper on the side—front zippers were considered by many to be too risqué.

The boy next door, about whom the girl next door might be talking on the telephone, was most definitely clean cut, his trousers perfectly pressed and his shirt collar worn with a tie. But he drew the line at gray flannel; that fabric belonged strictly to the older generation. On college campuses, male students wearing belted chinos with long cardigans or sports jackets walked to class in penny loafers or white buckskin laceups à la crooner Pat Boone.

Those who shunned the collegiate scene to follow Beat Generation figures such as Jack Kerouac and Allen Ginsberg donned dark, rough textures. Those caught somewhere in the middle—not quite ready to give up their clean-cut wardrobes, but not willing to embrace the mainstream wholeheartedly—simply wore their chinos crumpled and tie askew.

Like the randomness of first love, the particular identity that the teenager of the 1950s tried to express was ultimately less important than the act of expression itself. But the feelings of empowerment and escape engendered by doing something that might cause the older generation to wag a finger were as central to a teen's development as blue jeans were to a wardrobe.

Aftermath

With the exception of blue jeans, most of the teen fashions of the 1950s ran their course just as the leisure suits of the 1970s and the rubber gasket bracelets worn by Madonna-wannabes during the 1980s did.

Denim, for its part, is not only everywhere now but also comes in myriad variations. As a result of chemical and mechanical alterations, the fabric is available in bleached, stonewashed, sandblasted and overdyed conditions. Textile makers have also woven it into lighter weights for summer wear, combined it with polyester for wrinkle resistance and married it to spandex for a skintight fit.

Although, according to one estimate, jeans sales fell from 502 million pairs in 1981 to 412 million in 1998, their popularity seems far from fading.

STOCK CAR RACING

The drivers listened to car radios, nonchalantly used dashboard cigarette lighters and even competed in rental cars. Dust flew off the crude dirt tracks. This was stock car racing in the 1950s, when the legendary Tim Flock drove nine races with his pet rhesus monkey as a passenger and navigated through a cloud of sea gulls at the old Daytona Beach course. "There were feathers, guts and blood all over my windshield," Flock later recalled. "There were so many feathers it looked like it was snowing....They had no idea we'd be coming down there at 142 miles per hour."

The wild and daring early years of NASCAR (National Association for Stock Car Automobile Racing) carried more than a trace of the sport's colorful pioneers: tax-dodging, moonshine-running rabble-rousers of America's whiskey belt. These bootleggers jump-started stock car racing during Prohibition, pushing their factory-model Fords to the limit, tearing up red clay roads with revenue agents hot on their trail. With their souped-up engines, custom shocks and daredevil nerves, these "good old boys" transported booze from upcountry stills to towns and cities.

When they weren't bootlegging, the Appalachian hell-raisers were working on their factory-issue cars or racing them against one another, sometimes in cow pastures, sometimes on dirt tracks. Crowds would gather and drivers with fierce but friendly rivalries would bet on their cars. By the mid-'30s, dirt-track races were a common Sunday attraction, with promoters offering purses as big as $500. But as former driver Sammy Packard recalls, "It would be halfway through a race, and you'd see a car going out the gate. It was the promoter with the money."

The person responsible for organizing and polishing the image of stock car racing was promoter Bill France, who envisioned a governing body for the sport that would establish rules for keeping

The sand track of Daytona Beach (left), an icon of stock car racing's early days, gave way to a paved track (above) in 1959.

With cars overturning (opposite) or spinning out (top), and very few safety regulations, early stock car racing was a dangerous pursuit; two of NASCAR's first stars were Junior Johnson (above, middle) and Tim Flock (right, middle).

"There was nothing that could happen in my life to keep me from going to the race the next Sunday."

—*SMOKEY YUNICK, race car owner/ mechanic*

the cars and competition equal; provide insurance for drivers; and implement a point system that would culminate in a championship, later named the Winston Cup. NASCAR was incorporated in February 1948 with France as president, and with the guiding principle that race cars be in the same condition as when they left the showroom floor. He felt people would respond to races featuring cars that they could buy and drive themselves. Car dealers came to live by the "Win on Sunday, sell on Monday" slogan.

But the sport couldn't shake its moonshiner past so quickly. In NASCAR's first "strictly stock" race, at the Charlotte Speedway dirt track, winner/bootlegger Glenn Dunnaway was disqualified for having a wedge in the rear springs to stiffen them, an established bootlegger trick. Another driver/bootlegger, Junior Johnson, was making as many as four runs a night for his father years before being licensed to drive. Johnson recalls that "it was hard, dangerous, scary work." His years of running whiskey served Johnson

To survive early tracks like the beach and road course at Daytona Beach (above), drivers always had to be prepared to make repairs, such as straightening out crushed fenders (left); Cotton Owens (opposite, with son Everett) won the 1957 Daytona Grand National Race in a '57 Pontiac.

well when he started racing on France's Grand National circuit in the early '50s, but they also got him in trouble. Johnson was so successful with his all-out driving style on those dirt tracks that he became a special target for revenue agents. They caught him at his father's backwoods still in 1956 and sent him to jail for two years. "Junior Johnson was wild as hell," said race car builder Ralph Moody.

While the NASCAR rules brought a certain order to stock car racing, the sport was anything but predictable. Cheating and foul play were common throughout the '50s. Three-time NASCAR national champion Lee Petty, who would reportedly do anything to win, once used wing nuts and armor plating on the side of his Oldsmobile to shred the sheet-metal siding of his opponents' cars. One wily winner raised a post-race inspector's curiosity by having a warm engine but a cold cam, which would suggest that he had used an illegal cam during the race. He was awarded the victory just the same. As Lee Petty's son Richard,

the all-time leader in NASCAR wins, recalled, "If you wasn't cheatin', you wasn't likely to be competitive."

Over time, however, dirt courses were paved, cars were modified to enhance safety and performance and corporate sponsorships boomed. The old beach course at Daytona—where races had to be called for high tide and drivers spun out in the surf and got stuck in the sand—saw its last race in 1958. The new Daytona International Speedway track, built by Bill France, was paved, steeply banked and two-and-a-half miles around. Upon seeing the new track, Lee Petty said, "We knew stock car racing was never going to be the same again." He spoke for an entire generation of stock car racing pioneers.

Aftermath

NASCAR racing—already a billion-dollar business—is the fastest-growing sport in the country today. New multimillion-dollar venues in California and Texas draw enormous crowds. Even NASCAR's minor-league circuit, the Busch Series Grand National Division, attracts more than 60,000 spectators per race. Corporate sponsors spend more than $6 million a year to back Winston Cup racing teams, and more than 150 million people tune in to NASCAR races on TV each year. The 1997 TV ratings for NASCAR on ESPN were second only to National Football League games and were more than 50 percent higher than major league baseball games.

THE CAT IN THE HAT

In 1957 a debonair feline sauntered into the lives of young American readers and promised to show them "lots of good fun that is funny." Delivering on his promise, the Cat in the Hat, the literary invention of Dr. Seuss, has since introduced countless young readers not only to sounding out words and making sense of them, but also to the madcap and fantastic happenings that can unfold within a book's pages.

Given Dr. Seuss's enduring renown a as beloved writer and illustrator of children's books, it's hard to believe that by 1937, 28 publishers had rejected his first book, *And to Think that I Saw It on Mulberry Street*. At that time "Dr. Seuss"—the pen name of Theodor Seuss Geisel—was the signature appended to cartoons and humor pieces for such publications as *Judge, P.M., Life* and *Vanity Fair*. Seuss also designed an advertising campaign for Flit, a bug spray manufactured by Standard Oil, in which he

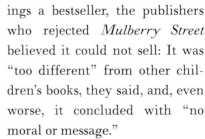

drew bugs with corkscrew noses and menacing grins that one of the company's executives complained were "too lovable to kill." Although Dr. Seuss's endearing illustrations had already been credited with making a volume of children's sayings a bestseller, the publishers who rejected *Mulberry Street* believed it could not sell: It was "too different" from other children's books, they said, and, even worse, it concluded with "no moral or message."

Walking along New York's Madison Avenue, about to give up on his book, Dr. Seuss bumped into a former Dartmouth classmate, Mike McClintock, who happened to have recently taken the position of juvenile editor at the Vanguard Press. Almost immediately after seeing *Mulberry Street*, the editors at Vanguard agreed to publish what Peter Rabbit creator Beatrix Potter described as "the cleverest book I have met with for many years."

Dr. Seuss's feline (opposite) made Sally and her brother (above) guiltless, though concerned, witnesses to his mayhem.

A modest success, the book unveiled the distinctive visual and literary sensibility of Dr. Seuss. With brilliant colors and bold, black outlines, the artwork radiates vitality, and the saucer-sized eyes of the animals in the drawings reveal their slightly manic, slightly dazed intelligence. The verse bounces along in lively meter and the story, like so many that would follow, develops through an accumulation of increasingly fantastic details that celebrate the wonder of children's imaginations.

After he had become known for such characters as Bartholomew Cubbins, Horton the Elephant and Thidwick the Big-Hearted Moose, Dr. Seuss was presented with a challenge. In a May 24, 1954, article in *Life*, "Why Do Students Bog Down on the First R?", writer John Hersey criticized the "uniform, bland, idealized and terribly literal" primers used to teach reading. "Why should they not have pictures that widen rather than narrow the associative richness the children give to the words they illustrate—drawings like those of the wonderfully imaginative geniuses among children's illustrators—Tenniel, Howard Pyle, 'Dr. Seuss,' Walt Disney?" asked Hersey. The question grabbed the attention of William Spaulding, the director of the education division at Houghton Mifflin, and in the spring of 1955 he met with Dr. Seuss to see if the writer could compose a story out of the 225-word list to which Houghton Mifflin limited its beginning readers.

Intrigued by the challenge, Dr. Seuss agreed to try. Later, gazing at the list, he discovered how few adjectives were on it, and that he could not write the tale he had in mind about a Queen Zebra, because neither "queen" nor "zebra" was to be found on it. Nevertheless, determined to make a title out of the first two rhyming words he found on the list, he saw "cat" and "hat"—and that was that!

"**Look at me!
Look at me!
Look at me NOW!
It is fun to have fun.
But you have to
know how.**"

—*THE CAT IN THE HAT*

A college notebook (opposite) showed the nascent style that allowed Seuss (right) to create an array of unforgettable characters.

Or not quite; it took Dr. Seuss an entire year to write and illustrate the book. In keeping with the then-favored "look-say" approach to teaching basic reading skills, he labored to maintain a close relationship between the book's illustrations and text—picturing nothing unnamed in the text and naming nothing not pictured. He also worked carefully with the vocabulary list, using rhyme and repetition to acquaint young readers with unfamiliar words. Dr. Seuss managed the task brilliantly, producing what Hersey proclaimed a "harum-scarum masterpiece" and proving that a limited vocabulary need not limit writers to the uneventful world of Dick and Jane.

While the tale does not begin with much promise—Mother leaves a young boy and his sister, Sally, alone at home on a day "Too wet to go out / And too cold to play ball"—the Cat in the Hat soon arrives to play "UP-UP-UP with a fish," a game in which he balances objects on his hands and his head while bouncing on a ball. After crashing and inviting his friends, Thing One and Thing Two, to add to the mess by flying kites indoors, the cat cleans everything up with a multi-armed machine and leaves just before Mother returns. The book, which allows children to participate in mayhem as guiltless, if concerned, onlookers, was an unqualified hit, selling nearly a million copies in three years.

Dr. Seuss was immediately invited by Random House (who published the best-selling noneducational edition of *The Cat in the Hat*) to establish his own imprint, Beginner Books. Through Beginner Books, Dr. Seuss enlivened the juvenile publishing industry and opened children's eyes to a wonderful world in which, as he wrote in *One Fish, Two Fish, Red Fish, Blue Fish*, "From there to here, from here to there, funny things are everywhere!"

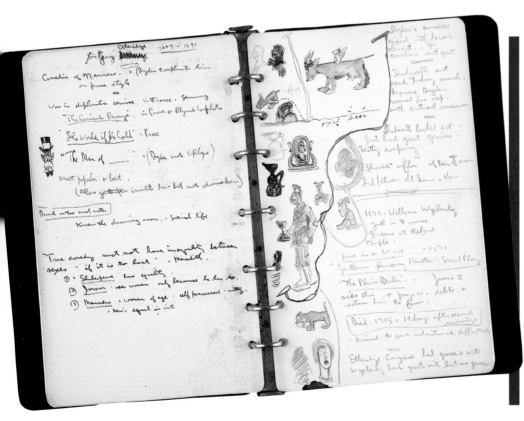

Aftermath

Dr. Seuss's most popular book may be *Green Eggs and Ham,* in which he limited himself to a 50-word vocabulary and hooked young readers with the stubborn and silly refrain, "I do not like green eggs and ham. I do not like them, Sam-I-am!" He also wrote picture books for adults, including *Oh, the Places You'll Go!* a favorite at graduations. He was awarded the Pulitzer Prize in 1984 for his revolutionary contributions to children's literature. Theodor Seuss Geisel died in his sleep on September 24, 1991, at age 87.

INDEX